CW01337405

JOHN ALDWORTH AND HIS PARISH

THE REVD JOHN ALDWORTH AND HIS PARISH OF EAST LOCKINGE

1684-1729

---

by JOHN COLLINS

Illustrated with wood engravings by Peter Collins

THE BLACK SWAN PRESS
WANTAGE 1989

ISBN 0 905475 14 3
Printed in England
at The Black Swan Press,
Grove, Wantage, Oxfordshire.

set in Monotype Plantin
and printed on *Revolver* long-life paper

ACKNOWLEDGEMENTS

I am very grateful to the following for their help in the production of this book: the Museum of English Rural Life, where I first started to study the original Aldworth Account Books and was given every facility to do so; the University of Reading (to which these Account Books were later transferred) for permission to make use of the Account Books and to reproduce a page from them; Christopher Loyd of Lockinge for his help and encouragement; and finally my son Peter for his major contribution – the wood engravings. The following have also been consulted while preparing this work:

The Berkshire County Record Office in respect of Lockinge Parish Registers, documents relating to John Aldworth's background and certain wills and inventories concerned.

The Public Record Office in identifying Frank Church in the Apprentice Registers.

Hallam *History of the Parish of East Lockinge*

Moorman *History of the Church of England*

M. A. Havinden *Estate Villages*

Mavor *Survey of Berkshire 1809*

J. S. Howse *Berkshire Probate Records 1653–1710*

The Agrarian History of England ed. Joan Thirsk 1984

John Richardson *The Local Historian's Encyclopedia* (2nd Edition) 1986

CONTENTS

List of illustrations *page* ix

Author's notes xi

1. THE SETTING Lockinge village: its manors, style of farming: population: the Aldworth Account Books: his family background: summary of farm accounts 1685–1715. *Appendices: 1. Sketch map* of *Lockinge, c. 1718. 2. Account Book headings. 3. Coins, weights and measures used in the Accounts.* 1

2. JOHN ALDWORTH'S CHURCH & RECTORY 1716–1729 Local farmers: his glebe: Lockinge church and its affairs: Rectory buildings: the Rector's servants: his sister Susanna Hester. 15

3. JOHN ALDWORTH'S STYLE OF LIFE IN OLD AGE Health: visits: horses: clothes: his outside interests: a story of King Charles I: the Rector's arrest. *Appendix 4. The Rector's clothes and footwear.* 31

4. THE RECTORY TABLE 1716–1729 General facts: wines: fish: meat: shellfish: food from local sources: fruit: poultry: food and beer consumed by household in 1725 as example: home slaughtering: fuel – coal and faggots. *Appendices: 5. Foodstuffs mentioned in the Accounts. 6. Household items.* 41

5. THE CHARITABLE RECTOR Local poor relief: Aldworth's personal charity and his priorities: educational charity: Frank Church: coats for poor men from tithe fleeces: briefs: passes: travellers: fire and flood. 55

6. THE FARMING RECTOR – ARABLE CROPS Overall profit and loss: crops grown – prices and buyers: 1718 farming calendar: wages: threshing and winnowing: disposal of crops: other farm jobs: detailed wages of taskers. *Appendix 7. Summary of farming Accounts 1686–1726.* 65

7. THE FARMING RECTOR – STABLE AND BACKSIDES Tenant farmers in 1718: cash flow problems: raising, slaughtering and preserving meat – pork and veal: cattle: poultry: fodder for stock: the village pound: horses: repairs to buildings: farm tools: thatching. *Appendix 8. Building materials: backside and stable – further details and costs.* 85

8. TITHES AND TAXES Tithe values in 1718: the Easter Offering: hay tithes: wool tithes. *Appendices: 9. Details of tithes and taxes paid. 10. Copy of 1718 Easter Offering.* 97

9. THE RECTOR LEAVES HIS PARISH 1729, Aldworth's last year: his will: his tomb and inscription on it. 107

Index 110

ILLUSTRATIONS

AUTHOR'S NOTES

A few matters which were commonplace to John Aldworth may perhaps be unfamiliar to some modern readers. These are given below and are essential to an understanding of the story.

The Julian Calendar was in use in England until 1752: at the time of the Reformation, the Book of Common Prayer fixed New Year's Day as the 25th of March, being Lady Day and the first day on which the world was created. The modern reader, accustomed to the Gregorian Calendar, must look out for different month numbers (e.g. '10 ber', meaning the tenth month, referred to December in those days) and for the fact that January and February were late months of the year. It is usual to make this clear by writing '15 Feb 1717/18' when meaning the 15th of February in the old calendar. England in fact adopted the Gregorian Calendar in 1752, 170 years after Catholic Europe. By then there was an eleven day difference between them and to put this right, the 2nd of September 1752 was directly followed in England by the 14th of September 1752. By a strange chance, a recent letter to *The Daily Telegraph* referred to this, adding that, about fifty years ago, the late Dr. Brittain of Jesus College, Cambridge founded UGBED – the Union for Getting Back the Eleven Days.

Coinage: As the whole of Aldworth's Accounts are recorded in pounds, shillings and pence, it is essential that readers realise that the pound sterling was then divided into twenty shillings, each of twelve pence and that each penny contained two halfpennies or four farthings. Since today's pound sterling is, of course, divided into 100 new pence, the penny relationship is not particularly simple: but a glance at some of today's small change will probably reveal an old shilling as being the same coin and value as five new pence. Having written this, I would advise against trying to change old values for objects into new currency. If comparisons between 1715 and 1988 must be made, it is generally thought that a larger sum – such as a yearly income – must be multiplied by about sixty to give some idea of its value in today's terms.

Measures: Few people today are in touch with grain measures. It is of some historic interest that these were measures of capacity, not of weight. The standard bushel of grain exactly filled a cylindrical container 19½ inches in diameter and 8¼ inches deep. By its nature, grain could be made level with the top (or, as it was said, 'stricken') but lumpy commodities such as fruit or coal could not be, and for these a 'heaped bushel' was allowed. Aldworth's grain was recorded in quarters, bushels and pecks which were thus related:

4 pecks	to	1 bushel
8 bushels	to	1 quarter

As a matter of interest, a bushel of wheat weighs about 63lb.

Coins and measures used by John Aldworth are given in Appendix 3, though these were not all standard throughout the country.

Farming methods: Although these are well known to anyone interested in farming history, I do not apologise for emphasising that the Rector lived in the days of total manual labour, with the help of tools used for centuries. Crops were hand-sown, hand-weeded, cut by scythe, carted by horses and finally threshed with flails and winnowed on hand-held fans. Small wonder that this took months to accomplish, and yet readers will also, I think, be struck by the economy and self-sufficiency of a small farming community.

CHAPTER ONE

The setting

THIS is the story of life at the ordinary level in a small farming parish near Wantage which was at that time – the seventeenth and eighteenth centuries – within the Royal County of Berkshire. It concerns some two hundred or so people ranging from labourers, craftsmen and smallholders to the tenant farmers and the Rector, who was himself a tenant farmer – no higher and no further. The evidence on which the story is based is both contemporary and detailed; most of it is derived from the Account Books of the Rector which will be explained in more detail later. They cover, in outline, the years 1685 to 1723 and in detail, those from 1716 to 1729; that is, they cover the whole of John Aldworth's rectorship of the parish of East Lockinge, but do so in far greater detail during the last thirteen years of his life; for this Rector died in office at the age of seventy-seven.

My sources are the Account Books themselves, the Parish Records of the times, and a number of other sources which came to hand as my own family ancestors were involved in the story. I am only too aware that evidence coming largely from how a man earns and distributes his money is both incomplete and possible to misinterpret; it can also be tedious, in the pursuit of each last farthing. But close scrutiny – and I have been examining these documents over many years – reveals information of great interest about ordinary life and lacks neither human frailty nor humour. But firstly the place and the people must be introduced.

East Lockinge is one of a number of parishes east of Wantage which are all strip-shaped, perhaps only a mile or so wide and six miles long, which extend from pasture in the north in the Vale of the White Horse, through arable land which finally rises to the Berkshire Downs to the south. Lockinge Parish, which has changed greatly in aspect since Aldworth's time, then consisted of East Lockinge clustered round its village church of All Saints; of the small hamlet of West Lockinge close by and of the hamlet of West Ginge, a little further off. Though wholely rural, Lockinge was far from isolated; the market town of Wantage was close by and the larger towns of Oxford, Reading and Newbury were within a day's ride. A main east-west route ran through Oxford and London, making a coach journey to the capital possible within a long day; Streatley, then without a bridge over the River Thames, had wharves handling barge traffic to and from London.

In the area of the Parish of East Lockinge, though not confined to it, were three small manors: East Lockinge itself, Betterton nearby, and West Ginge. All three were at the time in tenant hands. Lockinge, long held by the Keat family was, by 1716, held by a kinsman, Mr Prouze, and farmed by a number of tenant farmers. Betterton, another ancient manor, was the property of the Dean and Chapter of Westminster and tenanted by the Collins family which had, remarkably, held this tenancy in unbroken father-to-son descent from the late fifteenth century and were to continue to do so until the end of the nineteenth century: West Ginge's absentee landlords, the Hall family, had tenants – the Castles – who died out in the early eighteenth century, leaving tenant farmers in charge. Towards the end of John Aldworth's life, both East Lockinge and West Ginge were to be bought by an 'outsider', Matthew Wymondsold, bringing some changes to the village.

Local farming then followed the traditional style. Grain crops of wheat, barley and oats, with some beans and peas were raised; the wealthier tenant farmers grazed sheep on the Downs. Lesser folk were generally confined to smallholdings, varying in size, and to a share in the common fields; some kept a few head of cattle, and most a few pigs in the backside. The Rector held his glebe land, part of which lay in the common fields. As it so happens, this story looks at the last of the old agricultural methods in the area, of small, uneconomical farming by many tenants; although not enclosed by Act of Parliament until later, Lockinge was to be farmed in much bigger units in fewer hands. Betterton, however, had always been a single unit of some 500 acres and was to remain so. New farming methods, such as the seed drill and the introduction of root crops for winter feed were then (the early eighteenth century) only just emerging. Jethro Tull, one of the pioneers of new methods, farmed at one time quite close to Lockinge. Today, the village bears little or no resemblance to the one Aldworth knew so well. The cottages were then grouped, together with the Rectory, round the church, past which ran a stream – then called Copwell – which had not then been widened into an ornamental lake; the village road has also been diverted (see Appendix 1). Perhaps only two Lockinge buildings, though changed, have not been moved: the church of All Saints, which was then in a much simpler form; the other, lying a few hundred yards to the south-east, is the Manor House of Betterton, now almost completely altered, though John Aldworth would recognise the old barn and the ponds which had been dug by the Collins family earlier in the seventeenth century.

A study of the Parish Registers during the years of John Aldworth's ministry shows a slight rise in birth rate by the end of the seventeenth century, although infant mortality stood at one in every four live births. The village population in 1676 is known to have been 180 souls when a census showed them all to be of the established Church of England; this figure corresponds with a total of some forty to forty-five heads of families shown in the Rector's Easter Offering in the years between 1716 and 1729. There was considerable movement in and out of the parish but one would expect that from a parish of such narrow width. A few families were, however, extraordinarily tenacious; the Cullams, the Days, the Yates and, indeed, the Collins family of Betterton. Village people tended to marry young and to start a family at once; family size varied greatly but almost always was large enough to contain both boys and girls. Twins were of course rare (six sets between 1665 and 1729) and seldom lived for more than a few days. The average couple might have five children, of whom one would have died as a child; exceptions such as John and Mary Noke had three girls and eight boys, two others (twins) having died. To the great discomfiture of future genealogists, Christian names persisted from father to son and mother to daughter: John, Thomas and William for boys; Mary, Ann and Elizabeth for girls; these account for 60% of the baptismal names and make it impossible at times to differentiate between members of a family from the Parish Registers.

An act of 1678 required burial in woollen shrouds, thus promoting the home wool trade, and this was firmly upheld by the Rector of East Lockinge. In the Book of Affidavits almost all were buried in woollen, though with some few exceptions in the case of wealthier parishioners; £5 was levied in such cases, shared between the poor of the parish and the informer. Mr John Aldworth believed in leading by example and he was buried in woollen in 1729.

The Rector's Account Books, the main source of information for this story, concern themselves strictly with the running of the Rectory and its glebe lands; John Aldworth quite possibly had other financial resources but they do not enter his accounts. They reveal, as it were, a steward accounting for the running of a small concern, so that he may satisfy himself that it is being properly managed and the proceeds used appropriately.

At the start of each calendar year – that is on Lady Day, the 25th of March – he opened a new pair of folios. In one he recorded all receipts (he uses the Latin *Recepta*) as they occurred under appropriate headings; in the other he recorded all his expenses, again under suitable headings. Thereafter, he made entries in each 'book' until the end of the year, the 24th of March, and then totalled amounts under each heading. In the front of each book there is usually a form of *aide-mémoire* caused, at his own admission, by John Aldworth's faulty memory as he gets older. At the end of the year he transferred all the heading totals into a yearly summary book for both Recepta and Expenses. In order to give himself a true picture of his affairs, he totalled all his receipts, which generally consisted of tithe receipts and farm takings, and set against this total his farming expenses. This gave him what he called his clear profit. Finally he summarised all the rest of his Rectory expenses and thus arrived at an overall saving or overspending. (see Appx. 2)

The yearly account books survive from 1685 onwards but they, as has been explained, only give cash totals under the Recepta and Expenses headings. They only give, therefore, an idea of the Rector's progress as a farmer-manager and as head of his household. The detailed account books only exist from 1716 until his death in 1729 – and one or two of these are missing – but they offer a wealth of detailed information.

CHAPTER ONE

As already stated, there are dangers which must accompany a study of a man's accounts; one can easily draw false conclusions and make false judgements. I have therefore been at pains to avoid them and to express doubt whenever I have felt it. As to the character of John Aldworth, I will leave the facts to speak for him; he is for me an old and honoured friend.

Fortunately his Accounts are scrupulously kept in a fair hand which remains firm and clear until his last years. His spelling does not suffer from today's restrictions and is delightfully variable and often phonetic; it will be used deliberately whenever possible in this story. Readers are again reminded that the Julian Calendar was then in use, and should accustom themselves to the old currency of pounds, shillings and pence. Further details on coins, weights and measures are given at Appendix 3.

To understand John Aldworth at all, one must know something of his background. He came from a distinguished family: his father, Richard Aldworth (1614–80) was Auditor of the Exchequer at one time and, when not in London, lived on his estate at Ruscombe, near Hurst in Wiltshire, where six of his children, including John, were born to his wife Ann (formerly Ann Gwyn of Windsor). Having declared for the King in the Civil War, his estate was sequestered and a fine of £1,000 imposed on him by Parliament in 1649. But, as so often was the case, much lobbying and petitioning through influential friends eventually secured his estate – which his family had never quitted – and relieved him of part of the fine. John Aldworth, our future Rector, was born in 1652, the third to be born at Ruscombe. Susanna, the fourth child, who comes into this story, was over two years his junior. There were probably other children born to Richard and Ann Aldworth while they were in London. Various relations of the Rector of Lockinge are mentioned in his Accounts: one branch lived at Stanlake near Pangbourne in Berkshire, and a nephew of John Aldworth married into the powerful Neville family in 1714. A brother, Charles, died at Oxford in 1720 and another relation acted as his adviser in a tithe dispute which was settled out of court in Aldworth's favour in 1711. Indeed the name of Aldworth had been widespread in Berkshire for several centuries. These scraps of information are slight in themselves, but

No other light is shed on the matter nor were the normal events of John Aldworth's life disturbed.

Judging by his later harassment of John Aldworth's successor, the above may well refer to action by a newly-arrived Lord of Lockinge Manor, Mr Matthew Wymondsold, over some disputed ground or right of way.

Appendix 4

More Details of Cloth and Footwear from the Accounts

Material	*Description*	*Cost per yard*
'Stuff'	'any sort of commodity made of woollen thread &c. but in particular a manner those thin light ones that women make or line their gowns of or with.' (OED)	About 1*s.*
Shalloon	A light woollen stuff used for coat lining	Not known
Serge denim	Twilled cotton fabric with worsted wool	Not known
Kersey	A coarse woollen, usually ribbed	1*s.* 10*d.*
Calico	Imported cotton cloth	Not known
Holland	A coarse linen fabric	4*s.* per ell
Russel	Ribbed cotton/wool material	2*s.* 6*d.*
Popling	Corded fabric with silk warp and worsted weft	1*s.* 10*d.*
Broad durrance	A strong durable cloth	1*s.* 6*d.*

Examples of costs of materials and of making them up locally

Materials	*Cost*	*Made locally into*	*Cost*	*Total cost*
Cloth, shalloon, serge denim & buttons	£6 3*s.* 8*d.*	Coat & waistcoat	18*s.*	£7 1*s.* 8*d.*
Cloth, shalloon & buttons	£3 13*s.* 0*d.*	Coat & breeches	7*s.* 6*d.*	£4 0*s.* 6*d.*
7½ yds. cloth	£6 15*s.* 0*d.*	Gown & cassock	17*s.* 6*d.*	£7 12*s.* 0*d.*

Examples of complete cost of materials and tailoring

Winter suit	£5 11*s.* 3*d.*	Summer suit	£5 15*s.* 0*d.*
Drab suit	£5 2*s.* 6*d.*	Winter riding coat	£3 4*s.* 0*d.*
Crape gown	£2 0*s.* 6*d.*		

likes to think that, as contemporaries, they were friends who much respected each other – but that is pure conjecture.

The new Rector of Lockinge was as unusual for his times as was his bishop. He was neither poor nor ill-educated, nor was he ambitious for preferment; being a bachelor sharing his Rectory with his widowed sister, Susanna Hester, he could hardly be accused of having a large family. Events will show his keen interest in his parishioners and others, which was much encouraged by his position of farmer and priest; he dealt with all manner of men and women in his day-to-day farming life; with the local gentry, with corn-dealers and with the people he directly employed. There is a very healthy breath of democracy in his Accounts showing a labouring class well able to stand up for itself in spite of its poverty; it is also clear that the Rector greatly cared for those whom he employed.

His first thirty years at Lockinge are only covered by the Year Books mentioned earlier and these can be dealt with now, the evidence from them being both slight and generalised. The first striking fact is that, in spite of the inevitable fluctuations in farm income caused by weather and crop prices, the 'clear profit' of Aldworth's farming was practically always over £150 and averaged £230 over thirty-six years. Whether a modern accountant would wholly agree with the Rector's definition of a clear profit is doubtful as the expenses of building repairs, of the backside (mainly feed for cattle and pigs), and of taxes paid are excluded from this sum and come under the general expenses of Rectory living. Be that as it may, the main reason for the clear profit level was the low and unchanging cost of wages compared with the value of crops sold. Put in rather over-simple terms, a bushel of wheat was worth about four days of a farm labourer's wage. The clear profit, as will be seen, enabled the Rector to give well, to live pretty well, and to get about his parish duties. If he occasionally overspent, he had the necessary reserves from past savings to absorb some unusually high expense – such as £171 dispensed on repairs in 1697.

Only two other interesting facts emerge. On his arrival, and for the ensuing year, John Aldworth lodged with the Wisemans at a fee of £30 a year; Edmund Wiseman had become Lord of the

Manor of East Lockinge by marrying the last of the Keat family. By 1695 both the Wisemans had died without living issue, leaving the manor in the hands of Mr Prouze, a relation. The other item of some interest is that the Rector engaged a curate (unnamed) from 1686 for a few years, the starting stipend being £30 a year; this fell during the next two years, but to what level is not known as the stipend then is rather curiously aggregated with the wages of the Rector's maid-servant.

The fact that John Aldworth bought his wine from Portugal at this time is soon explained by the tariff preference given to Portugal by Britain following the Methuen Treaty of 1703. Claret had until then been the gentleman's drink, but during the wars with France it became a patriotic duty – and Aldworth was certainly a patriot – to turn to the lesser wines of Portugal; he may well have drunk claret in earlier days. Port – and John Aldworth refers to his wine as port – was then by no means the fortified and matured wine we know today; it was more probably on the thin side and not a good traveller, nor would it have lasted very long in cask or bottle. To illustrate this, a handbook of 1720 recommended that about three gallons of brandy should be added to a pipe (two hogsheads) of port during fermentation. The actual quality of the Rector's wine is of course not known, but he bought red port by the hogshead and white port by the half hogshead; with few exceptions he bought one of each every year between 1716 and 1729.

Although at that time it was normal for wine to be tapped from the wood into a bottle simply as a conveyance to the table, there is clear evidence that John Aldworth allowed his hogsheads to rest for a suitable period and then transferred all the drinkable wine out of them into his own bottles. Putting first things last, it may now be stated that his hogsheads came from London by barge to the wharves of Streatley-on-Thames where it was loaded onto the Rector's carts and hauled to Lockinge. Luckily Aldworth describes the whole process in some years, 1725 being typical; those with a mathematical bent may notice that 'bottle quantities' slightly exceed the hogshead capacity. This is soon explained by the fact that there was a necessary air gap at the top of each bottle as well as space for a cork.

27 May	Due for a hogshead of red port	£15. 0. 0
	& for Halfe Hogshead of white port	7. 5. 0
	& for cart hire	2*s*
	& spent in fetching it from Streatley	1*s*
28 Jul	pd Mr Ford for carriage of hogshead & ½	4 6
	& for wharfage 6*d* Given costbearer 2*s*	2 0
19 Nov	The ½ hogshead of white ran 29 gallons & ½ and filled 9 dozen and 4 quart bottles & 2 dozen pints.	

22 Nov The Hogshead of red port ran 60 gallons & ½. Filld 21 dozen, 8 qts, 5 pints fine. 15 pints foule.

Thus John Aldworth pays 4*s*. 6*d*. for the barge transport from London, 6*d*. for wharfage at Streatley and gives the bargemaster (or costbearer) 2*s*. Then, using his own horses, he hires a cart for 2*s*. for the last stage of the journey – which would have been an uneasy one for the wine. A full hogshead then contained sixty-three old Winchester wine gallons, which was slightly smaller than an imperial gallon. It is not known if John Aldworth had a cellar below his Rectory, though the 1663 inventory, referred to earlier, included somewhere in the house 'five great drinking barrels and three small barrels.' The reader will, however, readily understand why there was a bottle-house there. When the 1725 consignment had been decanted into bottles, no less than 362 quart bottles and 29 pint bottles had been filled. The bottles were then corked and for this the Rector bought corks from travelling saleswomen for around a shilling a gross, though this was open to bargaining. Only once is the purchase of new bottles mentioned when three dozen of them were bought for six shillings locally. The basic price of this wine varied a little over the years: in 1716 a hogshead of red port cost £15 but had risen to £18 in 1729; John Aldworth bought the latter only a month or so before his death. The half hogsheads of white port had correspondingly risen from £7. 5*s*. 0*d*. to £8 over the same period. If comparisons in cost have to be made, today's reader may like to know that the Rector paid about threepence per pint of wine.

Other mentions of 'beverages' are rare beside the forfeited brandy mentioned earlier. The Rector bought a hamper containing two dozen bottles of Canary wine both in 1724 and 1725, possibly for the sweeter tastes of his sister or his guests. The cost of each hamper, including carriage as far as Daniel Sayer's Inn at East Ilsley, was £2. 16*s*. 6*d*. Earlier there had been major repairs to the Rectory lead-lined wine cooler, including relining it with lead: this may perhaps have been used for the sweet wines. Nanny Hobbs, a Lockinge farmer's wife and a great provider of delicacies to the Rector, once brought him six bottles of burgundy; the only other beverage mentioned was a purchase of six quarts of cider. Wine

B. *Other expenses* which when deducted from the clear profit produce the Rector's overall saving or overspending for the year

Expenses of backside	Fodder and purchase of livestock
Clothes	The Rector's clothes, footwear, barber's bills
Private Expenses	Chiefly medical expenses and the cost of visits
Donations	Self-explanatory – including briefs and beggars from outside the parish
Taxes	Both Church and Lay (see ch. 8)
Reparations	To all Rectory buildings and the church chancel
Various Expenses	General Rectory living expenses
Wine from London	Cost including carriage
Extra Expenses	Buying and selling horses

Coins, Weights and Measures as mentioned in the Accounts

(see also the more general remarks in *Author's Notes*)

Coins: Aldworth's abbreviations are worth describing:

		from Latin
Farthing or a quarter of a penny	*q*	*quartus*
Halfpenny	*ob*	*obolus*
Penny or twelfth part of a shilling	*d*	*denarius*
Shilling or twentieth part of a pound	*s*	*solidus*
Pound sterling	*l*	*libra* (*ll* plural)

Frequently he omits these abbreviations altogether, using zero as a place keeper – sensibly when long columns of figures must be added. Thus '04.11.09*obq*' meant 'Four pounds, eleven shillings and ninepence three-farthings.' I shall use the modern £ sign in my text as the 'double *l*' used by Aldworth is confusing when typed.

Other coins mentioned

Groat	4*d*.
Guinea	£1 (but see below)
Broad piece	£1 3*s*. 0*d*.
Moidore	£1 7*s*. 0*d*.
Double pistole	£1 13*s*. 0*d*.

The value of the guinea, made of gold imported from New Guinea, was increased to £1. 1*s*. 0*d*. in 1717 and this is noted in Aldworth's Accounts. Harry Yates, who owed the Rector ten shillings (plus 1½*d*. interest) or half a guinea, 'paid not because guineas were by proclamation that day published at Wantage go for but 21*s*.'

Coins could also be used as weights. In 1721, after the death of his brother Charles, John Aldworth noted that two of his brother's silver spoons weighed two shillings and a sixpence of King William's coin and a groat of King Charles II coin.

Dry measure

Grain was measured in pecks, bushels and quarters; four pecks to end of December, there was a surprising reliance on smoked flitches of pork which were hung, as dried meat, until they were required; like pemmican, they had a good shelf life. Each flitch was half a pig's carcass and one or two were taken down for eating each month; it was not for nothing that country folk were referred to as chawbacons. In the same nine months, two calves were usually slaughtered, one in April and one in June, giving supplies of fresh or salted veal; in late November a steer was killed – though in almost every other year it was a bull which was fattened for slaughter. By December, the Rector's table had accounted for over £20 worth of butcher's meat; a barrel of oysters had been enjoyed, and a quantity of fish; both these in the spring. Mrs Hester had not been given any chocolate, but tea and sugar had been bought.

Accompanying the meat eaten in those first nine months of 1725 were over thirty bushels of the Rector's wheat for bread, pastry and cakes, and about the same quantity of malt from the Rector's barley was consumed as beer. A seventeenth century writer's opinion was that eight bushels of good barley malt produced:

'A hogshead (over sixty gallons) of "March" beer at the first brew for strangers. A 2nd hogshead of thinner household beer at the second brew. And a 3rd hogshead of thinnest small beer for plowmen and hind servants.'

This information suggests that the Rectory would have consumed 675 gallons of beer in nine months, but I doubt if that is in the least bit reliable.

Reviewing all these facts, particularly those about meat, we shall see later, in the chapter on Farming, what animals were slaughtered and when in order to provide the bulk of the Rectory's meat. In his old age John Aldworth seems to have taken a great interest in the whole process of bacon flitch production and the information he recorded was complete, as we shall see. Not so much is known of the preparations made for veal and beef; only the date of slaughter is given but we must suppose, I think, that much of such meat was butchered and salted away.

Although not within this chapter heading, I am now including the Rectory use of fuel, since much of it was used to cook the food. It has always interested me how householders of those and earlier days managed to keep themselves in wood fuel for all-the-year-round cooking and at least minimum winter heating: I can only assume that fallen wood was taken from standing trees and that hedge-trimmings provided kindling, but a village of some forty homes would, presumably, need a lot of timber. The Rector's Accounts do not really solve this problem; as he used coal he had, of course, less need for wood, but the fact that a mechanical jack was used for cooking in the kitchen suggests that wood was certainly used for that. Three chimneys we know to have been swept every year – for kitchen, parlour and study and probably the chambers above these. My guess is that cooking was done on a wood fire and that the 'furnis' for heating water was coal-fuelled, as were the reception rooms and some bedrooms in winter. Coal in quantity was then measured in chaldrons (or 'chadrons' in the Accounts); thirty-six 'heaped' bushels then officially making a chaldron. A chaldron weighed rather more than one ton.

The Rector's coal probably came from mines in the north-east of the country, then moved by sea to London – hence the expression 'sea-coal' – and thence by barge to Streatley in exactly the same way as did his wine. From there it was moved by horse and cart to Lockinge, and a very laborious journey this must have been on the country roads of those days. Readers with local knowledge will probably know that there was then no road up Bull Hill at Streatley – it would, anyway, have been too steep for cartloads of coal – and that the journey was by way of East Ilsey. With little variation the Rector ordered five chaldrons of coal each year in May and paid out costs which break down roughly as follows:

5 chaldrons delivered to Streatley at 27*s*. a chaldron	£ 6. 15*s*. 0*d*.
Mileage, lighterage, carriage and wharphage	2. 15*s*. 10*d*.
Hire of 5 horses & carts to lift coal to Lockinge	2. 0*s*. 0*d*.
	£11. 10*s*. 10*d*.

Apart from enjoying those '-age' endings, one notes that the carriage and handling of the coal cost little less than the fuel itself. These charges varied from year to year, though not greatly. Mr paid for servants as part of their offering. In Lockinge these amounted to about six who constituted what might be called the local gentry or yeomen; in general terms each farmed some five hundred acres, owned perhaps 250 sheep, and took a leading part in village affairs. Charles Collins of Betterton, though fourteen years the Rector's junior, probably knew him better than most. They were both Commissioners of the Land Tax, a task which took up a lot of time each spring, and both served on several local committees. Charles Collins had had two wives die young – a third was soon to die in 1723 – and John Aldworth had conducted the funerals of these ladies, and of no less than four Collins children of the nine he had baptised. A brother of Charles, John Collins, lived in the village and indeed died there some eight months after this entry in Aldworth's Accounts. (It may be remembered that he kept an *aide-mémoire* with them):

'12 Jan 1723. Mr Collins undertook my Curacy. The Wensday following (vid the 15th) he began His duties with reading Litany prayers. To have £40. I told him I would not offer less nor could I give more. He readily accepted it.'

It might be thought that the size and location of the Rector's glebe land would be known today, but it is not. There is much mention of field names in the Accounts but they are mostly names of a simple descriptive nature (e.g., 'the three lands just below Mr Collins' sheepshear') as opposed to accepted titles. It seems certain, however, that Barton Close and Barton Acre were enclosed pieces of glebe land; the former of some seven or eight acres was the plot on which a new Rectory was built long after, in about 1780, and which exists today. The rest of his glebe, to the best of my understanding, consisted of 'lands' or strips – the size of which is not known – in the common Lockinge fields. He, as well as others, had grazing rights on the Downs and at Laines (another surviving place-name) for his stock.

Fortunately, a list of land-owners and their holdings remains available for the year 1718, thanks to the raising of a small local rate then for church repairs. The land is measured in 'yard lands' which equate to acres in the ratio of thirty acres to one yard land. The manor holdings were as follows:

East Lockinge	2311 acres including West Lockinge
West Ginge	1090 acres
Betterton	510 acres (Confirmed by other evidence)

But there is, of course, no mention of the Rector's glebe.

His church of All Saints stands today, but in a rather different form. In 1716 it consisted of a fourteenth century chancel and a galleried nave with a three-decker pulpit; a twelfth century north door to the nave still survives. The same tower was there, housing probably five bells, and there was a south aisle dedicated to St. Catherine. Beneath the church were the vaults containing the remains of past lords of the three manors: the chancel vault for those of West Ginge, the east end of the south aisle for those of Lockinge, and the west end for those of Betterton. The repair and care of the chancel was traditionally the responsibility of the Rector. During those last years of Aldworth's incumbency he mentions in his Accounts quite a number of repairs to the chancel, and indeed to other parts of the church, carried out at his expense, including such well-used items as the churchyard gates, the altar steps and the altar rail. The gallery also needed attention and the Rector had the chancel wainscotted. In October 1723 Goody Moulden, a villager, was paid the large sum of five shillings for 'sounding in the Church'.

From various sources of evidence in the Rector's Accounts it is possible to establish the general form of church worship at Lockinge. It is certain that the Sacrament was taken on the great feast days of Palm Sunday, Easter Day, Whit Sunday, Michaelmas and Christmas Day. This we know because John Aldworth was in the habit of giving money to poor parishioners who attended; it seems likely that Holy Communion was held each Sunday as well, when a sermon was given and prayers read at evensong. Baptisms took place on Sundays before the whole congregation; though an infant might be privately baptised, by reason of frailty or fear of smallpox, it would later be 'admitted to the congregation'. Confirmations by the bishop were rare events because of the distances involved.

Poultry

Chickens	6*d.*–10*d.*	*General note*: These are probably live bird prices as the Rector kept his own poultry.
Ducks	2 for 1*s.* 6*d.*	
Geese	2*s.*–2*s.* 6*d.* e.	
Turkeys	2*s.* 6*d.*–3*s.* 6*d.* each	

Fish

Anchoves		*General note*: Excludes local fish (see local game). In 1725 fish was brought from Ilsley and from Titchfield.
Crab	9*d.* or 10*d.* e.	
Lobster	1*s.* each	
Mackerill	6*d.* each	
Oysters	3*s.* 6*d.* a barrel	
Prawns		
Salt fish		
Shrimps		
Sturgeon		

Beverages other than wine

Chocolate	10*s.* 6*d.* for an unknown quantity	
Cider	6 quarts for 1*s.*	
Coffee	About 4*s.* a lb	In 1721 a note reads: 'The first ½ of green coffee after it was roasted weighed 6 oz ½. This ½ pd of green coffee coud weigh but 7 oz: for the other weighed 9'
Tea		

Local Game

Dotterill	Brought to the Rectory by locals and 6*d.* usually paid. A lerk is, of course, a lark.
Hare	
Lerks	
Partridge	
Pigeon	
Rabbits	
Quail	
Woodcock	

Fish

Eels		
Ling		
Par		
Trout		Trout were frequently brought to the house.

Other foodstuffs

Bread	1*d*. and 6*d*. loaves	
Butter	6*d*. a lb	
Cakes	2 for 6*d*.	
Candid oringe peel	1*s*. for ½lb	
Cheese	5*d*. a lb	
Cheddar cheese	6*d*. a lb	
Cream	3*d*. a pint	
Honey	3½*d*. a lb	50lb bought once.
Lard	4*d*. a lb	
Milk		
Oatmeale		
Rice		
Salt	£1 a sack	For salting meat: not table salt
Trecle		

charity, was granted churchyard burial but not a funeral service because, years ago – the Rector's memory is sometimes far from faulty – she had only been sprinkled at baptism by a Presbyterian teacher and, continues the Rector in another marginal note, 'that without any necessity, I being then resident and my house and Church much nearer to the place of her birth than the Presbyterian's house and conventicle.' This suggests that there was a dissenting foothold in the area, possibly in Wantage.

After the church came the Rectory which housed John Aldworth, his sister Susanna, and two unmarried maid-servants – Mrs Hester's Martha was with her all the years from 1716 and was probably an older woman. A farm servant, Jonathan Atkins, also 'lived in' until his marriage in 1719. Quite a number of other villagers came and went doing various jobs about the house and garden but they were not regularly employed; some were fed at the Rectory, particularly when farm work was pressing, as at haymaking and harvest. What is abundantly clear from the Accounts, and will be brought out in more detail, is that the Rector very much looked after his own. It is immediately noticeable that all his workers were referred to by their Christian names and there is much evidence from elsewhere that servants at that period were regarded very much as part of the family, even if they 'knew their place'.

It may seem strange to describe the Rectory buildings, since they were totally demolished after John Aldworth's time, but there is plenty of evidence from the Accounts – principally from 'Reparations' – and I have also drawn on an inventory of the Rectory as it was in 1663; unfortunately there was no inventory with Aldworth's will and the one I used was attached to the will of William Page, a former Rector of Lockinge. The Rectory stood by the church with a forecourt and a vegetable garden: there was the main building with a few outhouses and, across a footbridge over Copwell stream, the backside with its barns and sheds. There was a well and also a cunningly constructed hand-pump, made by Thomas Robinson, a carpenter, which deserves mention:

'13 Apr 1716. pd Tho Robinson for boring 2 pieces of Timber for a pumpe, one of 10 foot, the other of 8 foot & putting in the said pumpe at 6*d* a foot – 9*s*.'

'pd Him for a sucker 5*d* & a pumpe spout 6*d*.'
The 'said pumpe' in fact gave a good deal of trouble over the years but was still in action in 1729.

The house itself was of brick with a tiled roof, both materials being obtained from local kilns on the Downs. The house was of moderate size with hall, parlour and study on the ground floor, together with kitchen and outbuildings; the last three of these rooms had fireplaces, the chimneys of which were swept every year, and the parlour chimney was fitted with a cowl to stop it smoking. The Rector installed a box-grate in his parlour, replacing the old andirons and firedogs, and thought it sufficiently noteworthy to put in his *aide-mémoire*. All these fireplaces and those upstairs were coal fired. The kitchen probably housed a furnace and a mechanical jack for turning meat before the fire. There was also a baking-oven for the Rectory bread, a woman being paid from time to time for 'heating the oven' – a task demanding a very early rising and much supervision before the loaves were baked. Among the outbuildings was a brew-house (the Rectory brewed large quantities of beer for its staff), a milk-house and a bottle-house, as the Rector did his own wine-bottling. There were two staircases – 'my sister's stairs' needing repair one year – leading to three or four chambers. The best ones, the Red Room and the Green Room, had fireplaces and the Green Room was fitted with a new freestone chimney-piece by a Wantage mason, John Kent, for fourteen shillings. There were small rooms for the two maids and one for Jonathan Atkins until he set up his own home. The Rectory had glazed windows, using either square panes or 'quarrels', which were diamond-shaped. Window tax paid by the Rector suggests up to twenty windows, but one cannot be sure as the tax rate periodically altered.

When lighting was required, the Rectory was candle-lit, using wax candles (at 6*d* per pound weight) in the best rooms. Elsewhere had to manage with home-moulded tallow candles made by the servants from the fat of slaughtered Rectory stock. John Aldworth's scrupulous payment and recording of his taxes allow one to have some idea of the Rectory consumption of candles, the tax being one penny per pound weight of candle. Nearly every year the two maid-servants settled down to making mould candles and in 1716 the

Rector obligingly tells us how many they made on the 11th, 12th and 13th of February 1716/17. They made 589, and in that year the Rector paid for '62pd' ('lb' is never used) in tax; thus we know that there were nine and a half candles to one pound weight – probably a seven inch candle judged from the fact that my five and a half inch candles are eleven to the pound. Over the years 1716 to 1729 the Rectory used just under sixty pounds, or 570 in number, in an average year, and these were not used in the best rooms. For these, wax candles were bought and also – probably used when the Rector was from time to time confined to bed by gout – rushlights and watch candles.

Furniture is seldom mentioned but, because the Rector arranged for their annual servicing, we know that he had two long clocks and a weather glass; Edward Keat regularly checked these, the mechanical jack in the kitchen, and Aldworth's sporting gun. A few other items mentioned are of interest: an alembic (limbeck) for distillation and a lead-lined wine cooler. Later in this narrative there will be many more examples of the self-sufficiency of a home or a community in those days – in the food and drink, the spinning, the weaving and the knitting; but it is appropriate now to meet those who worked for the Rector and his sister, for they were very much part of the Rectory.

Firstly there were the salaried living-in servants: these were the two maids, the Rector's earning £3 a year, and Mrs Hester's maid Martha who seems to have been paid as much as £10 a year. Not being paid by the Rector her wages do not enter his Accounts, but he once lent his sister £10 'for wages'. Both mainly worked in the house, but sometimes received the token harvest gloves which suggests that they helped with the harvest. Then there were the Rector's two male farm-servants; the first, paid £8 a year, one might call his bailiff on a small scale. He is the working deputy for his master on the farm, in the backside, at Wantage market, buying and selling stock and grain – a very busy man of whom we shall hear more, as he continues his job until his master's death. The second man-servant's duties also lay mainly in the fields, at an annual salary of £4 10*s*. Together they were the nucleus of John Aldworth's haymaking and harvesting teams.

All four servants were formally hired each year, paid in arrears and, if satisfactory, then re-engaged with the addition of a small 'earnest'. Each obviously had a clearly defined task, and if required to work outside it, they were paid extra; the maids, as we already know, were paid extra for moulding candles, as was the senior man-servant for slaughtering stock and the second one for brewing the Rectory beer. A general rule was that only unmarried servants lived in the Rectory; but all four were generously treated, their meals provided, medical expenses paid for (and these could be as much as a year's salary in serious cases), and their washing done for them. There were others who worked for the Rector who were paid by the day or by the job; they will be dealt with in some detail later.

The difficulty with the salaried servants is that, by this very definition, their normal work is not recorded in the Accounts; much more is known of the 'taskers'. Nevertheless a great deal can be deduced from the many entries which concerned the Rector's right-hand man whose name was Robert Absolom – always referred to as Rob. In 1716 he was probably about twenty-five to thirty years old, married to Ann (who came from Bensington in Oxfordshire) in 1711, with a boy and a girl; they had their own home in the village. Rob's work certainly included dispensing his master's money for the household expenses of the week. Whether he himself, or another servant, went to Wantage it was Rob who was paid by the Rector against a statement of purchases. Because of this arrangement, many detailed purchases are not known to us, the Rector paying the total bill as presented to him. Nan, Rob's wife, helped in the Rectory when she could spare the time from her children and she occasionally worked in the field; as will be seen, women did certain specific farm jobs. It was therefore a cruel blow when this young woman died in December 1723, almost certainly in a smallpox epidemic. John Aldworth paid the very substantial doctor's fees of ten guineas and Robert Absolom continued in his service. Earlier, Rob's children had already worked at the Rectory in a small way; Jack, the eldest child and only son, earned his first money dislodging rooks' nests and later, aged nine, he proudly led the leading horse bringing in the harvest. He continued to work for the Rector, and in 1725 when he was thirteen years old, he began working full-time during haymaking and harvest, earning the boy's rate of fourpence a day.

During the dozen years we are considering, John Aldworth carefully records the details of two occasions when he fell out with his principal servant. They deserve quotation, giving, as they do, some insight into the personalities of both men. The first occasion, in October 1717, concerned some wheat straw due to be delivered from the Rectory to Mr Price of Ardington. The *aide-mémoire* continues:

> Thu 31 Oct. After he had breakfasted and loaded 30 dozen of straw, Robert and I parted. I told him he was a confident fellow to carry the straw at once which I had ordered to be carried at twice. He answered gruffly (indeed as he answered me gruffly all that morning) that I might get my work done better I answered I would and he might go about his business. He immediately took up his clothes, went off, saying he would come no more.

In fact Rob did 'come more' and fairly soon after the incident; in the heat of the moment he had perhaps forgotten that his annual wages were due only a fortnight after.

Eighteen months later a very similar scene took place. Again the Rector, through his *aide-mémoire*, speaks for himself:

> 14 Apr 1719. Robert upon my bidding make haste to winnowing (the work he himself had proposed) told me he would go no faster: that he knew his work: that he had but little to do: that I was angry with him because it rained. All this in a rude and noisy manner. I answered he was a rude and ungrateful fellow: told him he did not know his business which was to respect his master: bid him go about it and leave talking: told him I could not be angry because it rained, having told Jonathan it was a blessed one. I might have added I had prayed for it. I have no ill-will to him in writing this – but I know the weakness of my memory.

Once more, Robert controlled his temper and went about his business. He had one more tiff with the Rector which only merited a short entry, albeit an incorrect one: 'Robert and I parted' in July 1724. It would be foolish to draw conclusions from these isolated master-servant quarrels: one can however say that there was nothing servile in Robert Absolom and that John Aldworth showed his concern for his own fairness towards a servant by the very act of recording these incidents.

In the years 1716 to 1729 three other men-servants appear in succession. Each is an unmarried young man and it is very difficult to be sure of their duties due to their salaried status. Jonathan Atkins was there in 1716 and certainly lived in the Rectory as various repairs to his chamber are recorded. In 1719 he married a Wantage girl, Mary Patience, thereby losing his 'all-found' job, but he at once took up the job of one of the Rector's taskers and continued in his service on a daily wage for most of each succeeding year. This allows one to make a very interesting comparison between his earnings as a servant and as a tasker. From a salary of £4 10*s*. all-found, Jonathan earned £8 6*s*. 5*d*. from his work for the Rector doing all manner of farm jobs but chiefly threshing and winnowing. On this money he and his wife raised a family of two children born in 1720 and 1722.

One of the second man-servant's duties, for which he was paid extra, was to see to the Rectory beer requirements. Most of the beer was no doubt for the servants and taskers as John Aldworth, his sister and any guests were more likely to have drunk wine. Jonathan brewed as demand arose, generally monthly, and stored his products in barrels in the brew-house. During the first few years the Rector bought the requisite quantity of malt from the miller and obtained hops either from tithe receipts in kind or by purchase; as from 1722 it seems to have occurred to him that it would be simpler to send his own barley to the miller and exchange it for malt at the rate of eightpence a bushel; a bushel of barley then being worth about three shillings. The miller – who is once named Billy Twilly by John Aldworth – did the grinding until the Rector installed his own grindstone. Duty of one penny a pound weight was payable on hops. The amount of beer brewed is not known, but Jonathan was accustomed to brewing either six or ten bushels once in most months, earning an extra day's pay for so doing: about three or four pounds of hops were used with six bushels of malt.

After Jonathan, as man-servant, came young John Cullum (or Cullam), son of Thomas and Elizabeth Cullum, members of an unusually large Lockinge family – so large as to deserve a mention at this point. Thirteen Cullums were baptised in Lockinge between 1685 and 1705: from the males of this number (including Thomas above) twenty-seven more Cullum children were born there between 1715 and 1737, all baptised at Lockinge. With such numbers an occasional lapse might be expected, and Martha Cullum, a cousin of John, gave birth to a natural daughter in 1715 and to a second in 1717, by which time, to quote the Rector, she was 'thought to be married' to an ex-soldier called William Bassett. Both children were baptised.

John Cullum was an impetuous young man. When he went to collect his year's wages, in October 1720, he was docked the customary harvest gloves because, as his master sternly put it – 'he went to a statute fair and left no man in his place' – not very fair on the others at harvest time. He carried on in the Rector's service only until the following June, when the following incident proved too much for John Aldworth's patience:

> Tues night 20 Jun 1721. I sent Jack Absolom for John Cullum from the Hobbs sheepshire He not coming, I went myself for him Asked the company if I had not a young man among them, seeing him striving with another. Asked him why he gave me the trouble to fetch him. He came towards my house but grumbling. I behind him bid him home. He answered he would not be drove home till he himself was minded and willing. I told him I thought I should know how to deal with him: then I went by him into my yard and so into the stable, the door of which I first locked up and then locked up the cart gates. He had full time to follow me if he had pleased. The next morning Martha told me he had gone away. This he did once before. Su Cullum says I said I did not care whether he ever came into my gates again.

This is the Su Cullum who had received a Valentine five years before; she was, of course, a cousin of John and was at that time working in the Rectory. Jack Absolom was Rob's nine-year-old son. The Rector was certainly not a bearer of grudges; he continued to employ several other Cullums and noted John Cullum's wedding in Wantage a few years later. The latter must have found new employment but he came back every year or so to have his old master baptise another child – and there were eight in all.

John was succeeded by Thomas Darter just two days after the incident; he continued in the job until John Aldworth died.

The exact duties of the maid-servants are equally elusive. Martha (her surname is never given) stayed with Mrs Hester throughout this period. She was probably an older, unmarried or widowed woman; there is one mention of her having a niece. The fact that Susanna Hester's affairs are obviously kept separate from her brother's suggests a business-like relationship between them which was not necessarily cool; she was remembered affectionately in the Rector's will and stayed on in the village after his death. She paid £30 a year, in equal quarterly parts, and paid interest once for being late with her payment; but again this was a normal practice as far as John Aldworth was concerned whenever money was lent or borrowed. She has both the means and the freedom to visit London and does so in 1716 and again in 1719: she is escorted by the Rector or Rob to and from Reading whence she takes the coach to London, very probably to stay with relations, and she is away for about a month. On both occasions she returned loaded with materials for her own wardrobe (one assumes) and also for that of brother John who duly reimburses her for such things as mohair, holland, calico, thread, stockings, muslin neckcloths and woollen socks. It was then the common practice in such circles to buy the necessary cloth, lining material, buttons and so on and to have them assembled by a local tailor. Little remains to be said about Susanna Hester and her maid; Martha, by deduction, not direct evidence, was almost certainly the Rectory cook as such work would not have been entrusted to a young village girl. Mrs Hester, for reasons not known, bought substantial quantities of lard from her brother every year – thirty to fifty pounds weight was not unusual – from the slaughter of his pigs.

The Rector's maids – there were four in succession from 1716 – were all young and unmarried, earning £3 a year or, in harsher terms, just fourteen old pence a week. But they had many advantages; the opportunity to learn housewifery before marriage certainly being one. Parents would welcome the girl's earnings; board and lodging was free and the master was a generous man. Typical of the four was, perhaps, Ann White, hired on the 2nd of

March 1716/17 when her predecessor left to get married. She stayed with the Rector for exactly seven years and the only duty of which I can be certain is that she was responsible for milking the Rector's cows – this because Thomas Darter had to be paid extra to replace her when she was once ill. She also caused one of the very few entries in the Accounts which shows how a servant could make a perfectly legitimate addition to her salary. Following the slaughter of some Rectory livestock each year, there was a large amount of lard, grease and tallow for disposal, as we know from Mrs Hester's purchase of some. In 1723 Ann bought fifty pounds of tallow from her master for 14*s*. 6*d*. (3½*d*. a lb); she then moulded the tallow into candles and sold back to the Rector exactly 14*s*. 6*d*. worth of candles (at 6*d*. a lb) leaving herself with some twenty-one pounds of tallow unused which, if sold elsewhere, would yield her a clear profit of 10*s*. 6*d*. She was the one servant whose laundry was not paid for by the Rector. 1723 was an eventful year for her. She fell seriously ill in a smallpox epidemic but recovered thanks to the attentions of the doctor, Mr Lockton, whose 'physick' cost John Aldworth 18*s*. 6*d*. By the following March she must have been fully recovered as she left the Rectory on the anniversary of the very day that she started there seven years earlier, to marry a young local man, Charles Cannon. She was given a very generous present by the Rector, no less than £1 4*s*. 0*d*., entered in the Rector's Accounts as 'for going to housekeeping' – as indeed she was.

Just as John Aldworth employed some casual labour in his fields, so were a number of village women employed about the house and garden. Firstly there was a great deal of washing to be done, of clothes belonging to the Rector, his sister and servants; two women usually tackled this work. Taking 1721 as an example, Goody Elizabeth Cullum was responsible for washing the clothes of Martha and of Thomas Darter; Nan Absolom (who believed in keeping business in the family) washed for her husband Rob. Both were paid half-yearly on the following curious scale:

Goody Cullum	for washing Martha's clothes	8*s*. per half year
	for washing Thomas' clothes	5*s*.
Goody Absolom	for washing Rob's clothes	7*s*. 6*d*.

Two other women helped in the Rectory: Goody Day weeded the garden and forecourt a few times in August and September, Goody Noke did the housework and scouring perhaps twice a month, and Goody Edmunds as well as washing had the unenviable task of picking feathers. Generally these women were paid 6*d.* a day, but a lesser amount if they were given a meal. Other occasional work for women included marking linen and napkins (1*d.* an article), carding, spinning, knitting wool, bottling wine and heating the oven (almost certainly to bake bread). As a simple example of payment, Goody Edmunds in 1722 carded and spun 2lb of the Rector's tithe wool for 1*s.* 6*d.* and from this wool knitted him three pairs of stockings for 1*s.* 6*d.* a pair.

Later it will be seen that women did a number of field jobs as well as work around the Rectory; it will then become clear why they were glad to have this occasional work – hard outdoor work – for half the wage of a man.

CHAPTER THREE

John Aldworth's style of life in old age

THE detailed Account Books cover the last years of his life, from the age of sixty-four to seventy-seven, and they show a steady – indeed expected – decline in John Aldworth's health and activity. He was increasingly crippled by gout.

This very unpleasant complaint probably started before 1716 but from then onwards the attacks were more frequent and prolonged. One may assume that, if Mr Price had to be called in to take the Rector's church services, then the latter was certainly confined to his house; either in bed or with his foot up on a stool. This situation began to repeat itself every winter during December or January, or both, for periods of a week or up to a month; there was relief from this in 1722 and again in 1724 and 1725 but thereafter there were longer fits of gout culminating in 1728 when Mr Price had to read prayers in Lockinge church all the year. The doctor's visits became more frequent over the years, as did the application of various medicines and salves. Balm, bitters, gum ammoniaci, alcaly water and spirits of carryway (I am using Aldworth's spellings) are mentioned. Electuaries were prepared, mixing ground herbs with honey and one locally grown herb, ground ivy, was collected. My medical knowledge is quite inadequate to suggest whether all these were cures for gout or any other ailment; no doubt much was based on Culpeper's *Complete Herbal* published in 1652. Probably it would have been sensible if John Aldworth had greatly restricted his consumption of meat and wine, but medical knowledge had not yet reached that idea. As we know, the Rector kept a 'limbeck' and once spirits are mentioned when he obtained no less than thirty-four quarts and one pint of 'forfeited Nants brandy' at two shillings a quart. The amount of wine and food consumed at the Rectory table will be considered later, but there is no suggestion that John Aldworth was a particularly heavy drinker. Apart from gout, he survived a nasty fall from his horse in 1717, a tooth extraction in 1726, and a blood-letting the following year.

In spite of painful disability, he continued to get about in his parish and beyond whenever he could; local roads would have been very difficult for travel in winter, gout or no gout, and John Aldworth seldom travelled far enough to necessitate an overnight stop. Once he stayed a few days in Oxford when his brother Charles died there in 1720, and as late as 1728 he went all the way to Stanlake near Pangbourne to see a nephew, Richard Aldworth. This Richard, who had married into the influential Neville family in 1714, later fought a duel at Stanlake after his own birthday party; one of his guests, Owen Buckingham, received so severe an arm wound that he died soon after.

Every spring the Rector was busy in Wantage, usually at the Bear Inn, with his fellow Commissioners of the Land Tax, choosing Assessors, and hearing appeals. His last appearance at this duty was just a month before he died. His Bishop's visitations also caused him to visit other places in the area once a year; it was at Wallingford in 1723 where he paid the Bishop 6*s*. 10½*d*. and spent no less than 10*s*. 2*d*. on himself. In the following year he was unable to attend, sending Mr Price as his substitute and allowing him 5*s*. 4*d*. 'for His dinner et cet'. There were other excursions on business; buying or selling a horse, consulting an attorney, but they tended to die away after about 1724.

As they incurred no money transaction, visits by others to the Rectory are not known, with the one exception of Elizabeth Aldworth's visit in 1718. She (as a good Aldworth) also kept expense accounts and had this to say on her visit to her uncle, probably accompanied by her own mother:

26 Aug	Going through a gate at Aston in the Oxford road	3*d*
	To a man playing the bagpipes at Tetsworth	3*d*
	To a poor woman at Wheatley Bridge	¾*d*
28 Aug	Given to Aunt Hester's maid 1*s* 3*d* To my uncle John's man	6*d*
29 Aug	To a man showing us Blenheim	1*s* 3*d*
1 Sep	Lodged at Oxford	

The journey, which was from Windsor, can easily be followed on a modern road map; Aston is near Henley and its distance from Oxford via Tetsworth and Wheatley is about thirty miles. Blenheim Palace had then only recently been built. As in the case just quoted, it was then normal to give tips for services rendered; even for short visits, a horse needed to be looked after, if not fed and watered. Thanks to this, we know of most of John Aldworth's visits but virtually nothing of visits to himself or his sister. As far as I have been able to find out, the Rector did not use any sort of a carriage; only once is a 'charret' mentioned, but my information is that this was in fact a sort of farm cart. That he rode a horse is in no doubt at all; not only are sales and purchases of horses frequent but John Aldworth's 'cloathes' include items specifically for use on horseback. Very careful study of all the Accounts evidence still leaves the reader unclear about the number of horses kept at the Rectory, and which are farm horses as opposed to 'nags' – as Aldworth always calls his riding horses. Firstly there is the evidence of Extra Expenses (or 'Ex Ex') which clearly shows the buying and selling of horses: there is no particular regularity to these; some horses are kept for years, others for a few months. They are, when bought, invariably colts or geldings, three-, four-, or five-year-olds and are described in some detail in the Accounts such as:

> 2 Mar 1717. bought a 3 year old or come 3 year old colt for £12.15.0
> It was a black colt with a small star & one white foote behinde.

And in 1726, only three years before he died he bought two horses and sold two others:

Oct 28. Bought at Newburrough A come 3 year old for	£12.13.0
& a come foare year old for	11.14.0
spent in buying them	0. 2.0
Both had White feet, stars & some white on their noses	
Ex receits	
July 28	
Oct 15 Sold Moon blinde for	9. 0.0
March 11 of Rob for old Blind & broken winde	2. 0.0

Other evidence, to which we shall come when considering the Rector's farm, suggests that he kept four or five horses, one of which was his personal nag. As happens in the best equestrian circles, John Aldworth had occasional difficulties with his nags. Just before Easter in 1717 he took a nasty fall from his horse. The whole affair was as expensive as it was painful: not only did he need Mr Lockton to attend him (ten shillings) but Mr Price had to preach for him on Easter Sunday (ten shillings) and Thomas Batten's men had to be given two shillings for catching the animal.

Next year John Aldworth had to compensate a local man, John Weden, 'my nag having lamed his mare' and though no proof exists, suspicion falls on a certain Thin Guts, a three-year-old gelding bought in 1716. The Rector had twice tried to sell the horse; Mr Price hurriedly returned it after one day's trial and got his money back. Next year another would-be purchaser was not so lucky; although he returned the dreadful Thin Guts equally quickly, he lost his 'earnest' or, as would now be said, his deposit of one guinea.

Expenditure on the Rector's 'cloathes' are interesting in themselves and show, as in the example above, that between fits of gout he continued to lead an active outdoor life in old age.

Starting at the top, John Aldworth invariably wore under his clerical hat a periwig, buying one or two every year. For this purpose he needed to keep his hair short and this was attended to by Mr Mills who also made his periwigs. However in 1724, after a trial trim the previous Christmas, the Rector engaged Richard Toms for this service:

'6 Oct. Rich Toms trimd me. He is to shave me once a week and to have halfe a Guinny for the ensuing halfe yeare.' And from then on, both Mr Mills and Rich Toms continued to serve the Rector. Appropriately, Rich Toms was the village thatcher.

Rectory linen was made up at home from bought materials either ordered from London or, as already shown, brought back from a visit there by his sister. The local tailor was Thomas Kimber who not only mended garments but made up new ones from the material bought. The fact that John Aldworth bought two or three pairs of shoes every year, supplied by a Mr Butcher, suggests an active pedestrian life; stockings were normally knitted at home from the wool of tithe fleeces and gloves made locally from the skins of slaughtered Rectory calves. John Aldworth had, as we know, his top clothes made up locally and he continued to do so steadily until he bought his last drab suit in 1727. Up till then he had a new riding coat, waistcoat and pair of breeches almost every year: his last camlet riding coat was made up in 1724 after which he went in more for suits – for both winter and summer. When it came to chilly Berkshire nights, Thomas Kimber kept him well supplied with nightcaps. Further details of materials bought and their costs are given in Appendix 4, together with the costs of making them up into clothes, where known.

In his old age, and no doubt all his life, the Rector kept up a lively interest in affairs beyond his parish from reading books, news-sheets, letters from friends and relations and, on at least one occasion, from local gossip. This last was important enough to John Aldworth to include in his *aide-mémoire* and for me to include now:

> 15 Apr 1722. Mr Johnson told me He could tell me what He thout I knew not. It was yt when King Charles was prisoner in the Ile of Wight cromwell offerd to restore Him to His throne: this he did by some other person. The K before he consented wrote to the Queen. She returned an answer that He should agree to it: That she woud certainly poyson the rogue afterwards: This letter He said was spirited up by the Cardinal. Cromwell had the first view of it & resolved to take Him off. Mr Johnson had said before yt the cardinal ownd He had raised up a spirit He could not lay. The letter showd He intended to keep up the flame and encrease not extinguish it. If this story was true (and He said He had seen the Ks and Queens letters) the Ks blood lay at Hers and Mazarines dores.

Mr Johnson, who passed on his story some seventy-five years after the events in it, cannot be identified. But the gist of the story – which is not particularly easy to follow – seems to be this:

While King Charles I was imprisoned in Carisbrooke Castle on the Isle of Wight from November 1647 to December 1648, Cromwell wrote to him, through an intermediary, offering to restore the King to his throne. Before agreeing to this, King Charles consulted his wife, Queen Henrietta, who replied advising acceptance, though she would have Cromwell poisoned afterwards. Mr Johnson believed that Cardinal Mazarin, France's all-powerful Minister, was behind the Queen's plan and that he later admitted that he had started something he could not stop. His involvement shows that he had no intention of stopping it, and the Queen's reply suggests that both the Cardinal and Queen Henrietta were in effect accomplices to the death of King Charles. John Aldworth's reflection was perhaps to doubt the truth of the story, but Mr Johnson said he had seen both the letters concerned.

There had been some suppression of public information during the Restoration and beyond, but by 1716 it had been freed and there is much evidence of John Aldworth's interest in the current affairs of the day. Up to 1722 there is regular mention of a monthly publication costing 6*d.* and referred to as 'Mer' or 'Mercury'; it was probably a London news-sheet entitled *Mercurius Politicus.* He also took what he simply calls 'News' at 1½*d.* a copy. There are frequent payments for letters and some of John Aldworth's letters have survived – in particular a series relating to a local tithe dispute with his friend and neighbour Mr Munt, a local tenant farmer. For this, the Rector invoked the heavy guns of a London attorney who was also his kinsman and the suit was settled out of court in 1711, in Aldworth's favour. His letters are more interesting for their comment on international affairs than for the actual suit itself and one letter to a relative deserves partial quotation. In it he refers to the negotiations which finally led to the Treaty of Utrecht after Marlborough's continental victories:

> 15 Dec 1711. I have received . . . your last two letters: in the first of which you sent me the Queen's most admirable speech: and in the other, the Commons very loyal address, with Her Majesty's most gracious answer. I look upon the Queen to be incomparably greater in that noble Corona of Church peers about her and her dutyful Commons before her, than in all the celebrated successes of her Arms. Of these, foreigners or subjects little better affected to our Constitution than they, reaped all the advantage from this, under God, we may promise to old England a peculiar and lasting happiness. . . . The satisfaction I take is in the prosperity of our private affairs: I do assure you that I am exceedingly pleased to find you so zealous for the interest of the Church and Crown and that you are still so much in the favour of His Grace the Duke of Northumberland as that he vouchsafes to continue franking your letters – to your most affectionate kinsman and humble servant – J.A.
> I thank you for your kind present: they fit. My sister is your servant.

One can almost see Susanna Hester asking the Rector if he had thanked him properly for his present – very likely a pair of knitted stockings.

Some idea of his taste in books comes from a number of entries in his *aide-mémoire* recording the lending of books – usually to Mr Price of Ardington. He lent two to him in 1722, both written by Fellows of All Souls, Aldworth's College, but expressing very different opinions. The first was Tindal's *Rights of the Christian Church asserted against the Romish and all other priests who claim an independent power over it* (A prodigious title, but the gist of its contents seems fairly evident). Tindal was a contemporary of John Aldworth at Oxford and, though trained as a lawyer, he took to making outspoken attacks on High Church attitudes. The book was published in 1706 and was sufficiently sensational as to cause authority to have it burnt four years later. The second book was based on an earlier one by Spinoza which was translated into English in 1689. *Spinoza Revived* came out in 1709 as an open answer to *Rights of the Christian Church.*

Other books mentioned by Aldworth were Dr Hicks' *Jovian* and *Quesnel on the Gospels*: later, after his brother's death in Oxford in 1720, John Aldworth took over a number of his books – thus requiring a new book press in the hall – including *The Practical Divinity of Papists destructive of Christianity* and Lassells's *Travels over Italy*.

It does not require deep study of these volumes to conclude that the Rector was a learned theologian who was also well informed about public affairs. There remains one curious – and as yet unexplained – event in his later life. In 1718 the following entries occur in the Expenses:

Private Ex

17 May	The Sherriff's Bayliff for arresting me	2*s*.
	At Wantage	1*s*. 9*d*.

Ex Ex

8 Sep	pd Clement the Bayly arresting me	2*s*.

No other light is shed on the matter nor were the normal events of John Aldworth's life disturbed.

Judging by his later harassment of John Aldworth's successor, the above may well refer to action by a newly-arrived Lord of Lockinge Manor, Mr Matthew Wymondsold, over some disputed ground or right of way.

Appendix 4

More Details of Cloth and Footwear from the Accounts

Material	*Description*	*Cost per yard*
'Stuff'	'any sort of commodity made of woollen thread &c. but in particular a manner those thin light ones that women make or line their gowns of or with.' (OED)	About 1*s.*
Shalloon	A light woollen stuff used for coat lining	Not known
Serge denim	Twilled cotton fabric with worsted wool	Not known
Kersey	A coarse woollen, usually ribbed	1*s.* 10*d.*
Calico	Imported cotton cloth	Not known
Holland	A coarse linen fabric	4*s.* per ell
Russel	Ribbed cotton/wool material	2*s.* 6*d.*
Popling	Corded fabric with silk warp and worsted weft	1*s.* 10*d.*
Broad durrance	A strong durable cloth	1*s.* 6*d.*

Examples of costs of materials and of making them up locally

Materials	*Cost*	*Made locally into*	*Cost*	*Total cost*
Cloth, shalloon, serge denim & buttons	£6 3*s.* 8*d.*	Coat & waist-coat	18*s.*	£7 1*s.* 8*d.*
Cloth, shalloon & buttons	£3 13*s.* 0*d.*	Coat & breeches	7*s.* 6*d.*	£4 0*s.* 6*d.*
7½ yds. cloth	£6 15*s.* 0*d.*	Gown & cassock	17*s.* 6*d.*	£7 12*s.* 0*d.*

Examples of complete cost of materials and tailoring

Winter suit	£5 11*s.* 3*d.*	Summer suit	£5 15*s.* 0*d.*
Drab suit	£5 2*s.* 6*d.*	Winter riding coat	£3 4*s.* 0*d.*
Crape gown	£2 0*s.* 6*d.*		

Cost of other items

Periwig	£1 2*s*. 6*d*.	Boots (a pair)	15*s*.
Wash-leather gloves	1*s*. 2*d*.	Shoes (a pair)	4*s*.–4*s*. 6*d*.
		Stockings (a pair)	3*s*.–4*s*. bought
Cotton nightcap	1*s*. 6*d*.		1*s*. 6*d*. home spun
Hat	10*s*.–14*s*.		
Socks (a pair)	6*d*.		

CHAPTER FOUR

The Rectory table 1716-1729

THE Expenditure heading 'Varied Expenses' contains almost all the evidence about the food eaten at the Rectory, but this needs to be treated warily. In the first place one must remember that the Rector fed many more mouths than his own and his sister's; it is not possible to sort out in any way 'who ate what' – only to assume that luxuries, such as oysters, were more likely to go to the Rector and his guests. Nor do we know how many guests he had and how often he entertained his friends and neighbours. The second difficulty is that the Account entries do not spell out every detail of what food is bought. John Aldworth paid Rob Absolom weekly against a list of what the latter had bought on his behalf; many entries therefore use the Latin tag *ut pt* or *ut paret* meaning that Aldworth had been shown the list and had paid for it *in toto*. Thus 'pd Nan 3*s*. 7*d*. *ut pt*' tells the reader nothing of her purchases: other entries may tell part of the story, e.g. 'pd Rob for bread, butter, roots, spent *ut pt* 1*s*. 11*d*.'. I have added at Appendix 5 a full list of every item mentioned in the Accounts, believing that there will be 'something for everybody' in this method, and the above will show the reader that the price of an article cannot always be given. In Appendix 6 a similar list of household items is mentioned.

'Varied Expenses' also included the quarterly butcher's bill which, one can only assume, contained delicacies or changes from the rather monotonous Rectory meat diet met by home-slaughtering of stock; it also contained the quantity of wheat used quarterly for Rectory bread: the slaughter and butchering of stock, and lastly the amount of malt and hops used for brewing. As from 1700, 'Wine' became a separate heading of expenditure, so that we are lucky to have a lot of detail on this subject from 1716 onwards. The Rector's wines will therefore be considered first and, though it is not known as a fact, I do not think it was the practice then for the Rector to provide Communion wine from his own purse.

The fact that John Aldworth bought his wine from Portugal at this time is soon explained by the tariff preference given to Portugal by Britain following the Methuen Treaty of 1703. Claret had until then been the gentleman's drink, but during the wars with France it became a patriotic duty – and Aldworth was certainly a patriot – to turn to the lesser wines of Portugal; he may well have drunk claret in earlier days. Port – and John Aldworth refers to his wine as port – was then by no means the fortified and matured wine we know today; it was more probably on the thin side and not a good traveller, nor would it have lasted very long in cask or bottle. To illustrate this, a handbook of 1720 recommended that about three gallons of brandy should be added to a pipe (two hogsheads) of port during fermentation. The actual quality of the Rector's wine is of course not known, but he bought red port by the hogshead and white port by the half hogshead; with few exceptions he bought one of each every year between 1716 and 1729.

Although at that time it was normal for wine to be tapped from the wood into a bottle simply as a conveyance to the table, there is clear evidence that John Aldworth allowed his hogsheads to rest for a suitable period and then transferred all the drinkable wine out of them into his own bottles. Putting first things last, it may now be stated that his hogsheads came from London by barge to the wharves of Streatley-on-Thames where it was loaded onto the Rector's carts and hauled to Lockinge. Luckily Aldworth describes the whole process in some years, 1725 being typical; those with a mathematical bent may notice that 'bottle quantities' slightly exceed the hogshead capacity. This is soon explained by the fact that there was a necessary air gap at the top of each bottle as well as space for a cork.

27 May	Due for a hogshead of red port	£15. 0. 0
	& for Halfe Hogshead of white port	7. 5. 0
	& for cart hire	2*s*
	& spent in fetching it from Streatley	1*s*
28 Jul	pd Mr Ford for carriage of hogshead & ½	4 6
	& for wharfage 6*d* Given costbearer 2*s*	2 0
19 Nov	The ½ hogshead of white ran 29 gallons & ½ and filled 9 dozen and 4 quart bottles & 2 dozen pints.	

22 Nov The Hogshead of red port ran 60 gallons & $\frac{1}{2}$. Filld 21 dozen, 8 qts, 5 pints fine. 15 pints foule.

Thus John Aldworth pays 4*s*. 6*d*. for the barge transport from London, 6*d*. for wharfage at Streatley and gives the bargemaster (or costbearer) 2*s*. Then, using his own horses, he hires a cart for 2*s*. for the last stage of the journey – which would have been an uneasy one for the wine. A full hogshead then contained sixty-three old Winchester wine gallons, which was slightly smaller than an imperial gallon. It is not known if John Aldworth had a cellar below his Rectory, though the 1663 inventory, referred to earlier, included somewhere in the house 'five great drinking barrels and three small barrels.' The reader will, however, readily understand why there was a bottle-house there. When the 1725 consignment had been decanted into bottles, no less than 362 quart bottles and 29 pint bottles had been filled. The bottles were then corked and for this the Rector bought corks from travelling saleswomen for around a shilling a gross, though this was open to bargaining. Only once is the purchase of new bottles mentioned when three dozen of them were bought for six shillings locally. The basic price of this wine varied a little over the years: in 1716 a hogshead of red port cost £15 but had risen to £18 in 1729; John Aldworth bought the latter only a month or so before his death. The half hogsheads of white port had correspondingly risen from £7. 5*s*. 0*d*. to £8 over the same period. If comparisons in cost have to be made, today's reader may like to know that the Rector paid about threepence per pint of wine.

Other mentions of 'beverages' are rare beside the forfeited brandy mentioned earlier. The Rector bought a hamper containing two dozen bottles of Canary wine both in 1724 and 1725, possibly for the sweeter tastes of his sister or his guests. The cost of each hamper, including carriage as far as Daniel Sayer's Inn at East Ilsley, was £2. 16*s*. 6*d*. Earlier there had been major repairs to the Rectory lead-lined wine cooler, including relining it with lead: this may perhaps have been used for the sweet wines. Nanny Hobbs, a Lockinge farmer's wife and a great provider of delicacies to the Rector, once brought him six bottles of burgundy; the only other beverage mentioned was a purchase of six quarts of cider. Wine was not the only commodity to reach Lockinge via the Streatley wharves; coal came to the Rectory by the same route and will be discussed at the end of this chapter.

Although such luxuries as oysters, sturgeon and chocolate catch the eye among the many purchases under 'Varied Expenses', they are very much the exception. John Aldworth certainly ate well, but he was not a gourmand and we know nothing of the actual dishes which were set before him – only a certain amount about the ingredients. Sturgeon was but a single entry; the chocolate, mentioned twice, was a present for his sister to drink; but one must admit that the Rector had a partiality for oysters which only left him in his last years. Unfortunately we do not know where they came from, but they arrived in barrels (at 3*s.* 6*d.* each) and were bought in the winter months. It is much more typical of the Rectory diet to relate its monotony than its special dishes and it is fairly certain that John Aldworth had his share of the monotony with his household.

The basic food then was meat, often salted or smoked, bread and beer; all this was home-grown and prepared for the table at the Rectory. The Rector himself, his sister and his guests would however have had the benefit of the wine, the butcher's meat and occasional gifts of game, including venison; not only did he do a little rough-shooting, but often a neighbour would bring him locally found wild animals and fish. Boys who were probably useful with the snare would provide small game and be given 6*d.* for their efforts; sometimes their produce was open to doubt – though in the case I quote I am surprised at a country parson's ignorance:

'1 Aug 1723 pd for a Hare (I think it a Rabbit) from young William George 1*s.*'

Trout was often fished or tickled from the local streams; on one occasion in 1718, Rob Absolom was paid an extra shilling for 'going fishing by night' but why, or with what result, is not known. Other game brought to the Rectory included partridge, quail, larks, woodcock and dotterel; the last named perhaps being the more common plover. If game came to the Rectory door, it would certainly have come to many others, and this source of food for village people was one of the advantages of unenclosed land, such as the Downs above Lockinge. Aldworth, like everyone else, had his vegetable garden and was in the habit of ordering eleven shillings' worth of 'garden stuff' every year, which suggests a fairly large plot; the evidence of one year is that 'garden stuff' was probably colewort or cabbage. A good deal of fruit was grown in Lockinge, mostly by the farmers; no need for the Rector to do this as he took fruit as a tithe from those parishioners who sold their own. Though naturally seasonal, there was quite a variety of local fruit: apples, pears, plums, cherries, gooseberries and walnuts and also rarer fruits such as quince, mulberry and apricot. From elsewhere came oranges and lemons, much used by the Rectory, and also figs. It is, I think, surprising that fruit is mentioned among 'Varied Expenses' in almost every month of the year. Tithes will be dealt with later, but as well as fruit, the Rector took other eatables such as eggs and pigeons as tithes; the Rectory backsides provided not only home-grown meat from cattle and pigs – these will be discussed under farming activities – but poultry, milk and cream. Whether or not it raised a smile at the time, the following entry in the Accounts deserves quotation:

'5 Aug 1726 pd Dame Mallard for 2 ducks 1*s.* 6*d.*'

There is no evidence of a turkey having been traditional Christmas fare but a Michaelmas goose was sometimes taken.

I have by no means mentioned every item of food used at the Rectory but, because it is certainly interesting, a full list is given at the end of the chapter (Appendix 5), giving the cost when that could be determined. A reminder is perhaps necessary that it is not possible to differentiate between the Rector's personal table and that of his servants and workers.

The basic diet enjoyed by the Rector's household was, as stated, monotonous; but the village worker in those days would hardly have complained of that – he would have thanked his God for a reasonably full stomach every day. To illustrate this, 1725 has been chosen as a typical year in which the records for this subject are particularly complete. The year, of course, started in late March, roughly coinciding with the agricultural cycle, with a spring sowing. Thus it was that the Rector employed most men during the spring and early summer, culminating in haymaking and harvest in high summer, when the Rectory was feeding most mouths.

Taking these first three quarters of the year, from March to the end of December, there was a surprising reliance on smoked flitches of pork which were hung, as dried meat, until they were required; like pemmican, they had a good shelf life. Each flitch was half a pig's carcass and one or two were taken down for eating each month; it was not for nothing that country folk were referred to as chawbacons. In the same nine months, two calves were usually slaughtered, one in April and one in June, giving supplies of fresh or salted veal; in late November a steer was killed – though in almost every other year it was a bull which was fattened for slaughter. By December, the Rector's table had accounted for over £20 worth of butcher's meat; a barrel of oysters had been enjoyed, and a quantity of fish; both these in the spring. Mrs Hester had not been given any chocolate, but tea and sugar had been bought.

Accompanying the meat eaten in those first nine months of 1725 were over thirty bushels of the Rector's wheat for bread, pastry and cakes, and about the same quantity of malt from the Rector's barley was consumed as beer. A seventeenth century writer's opinion was that eight bushels of good barley malt produced:

'A hogshead (over sixty gallons) of "March" beer at the first brew for strangers. A 2nd hogshead of thinner household beer at the second brew. And a 3rd hogshead of thinnest small beer for plowmen and hind servants.'

This information suggests that the Rectory would have consumed 675 gallons of beer in nine months, but I doubt if that is in the least bit reliable.

Reviewing all these facts, particularly those about meat, we shall see later, in the chapter on Farming, what animals were slaughtered and when in order to provide the bulk of the Rectory's meat. In his old age John Aldworth seems to have taken a great interest in the whole process of bacon flitch production and the information he recorded was complete, as we shall see. Not so much is known of the preparations made for veal and beef; only the date of slaughter is given but we must suppose, I think, that much of such meat was butchered and salted away.

Although not within this chapter heading, I am now including the Rectory use of fuel, since much of it was used to cook the food. It has always interested me how householders of those and earlier days managed to keep themselves in wood fuel for all-the-year-round cooking and at least minimum winter heating: I can only assume that fallen wood was taken from standing trees and that hedge-trimmings provided kindling, but a village of some forty homes would, presumably, need a lot of timber. The Rector's Accounts do not really solve this problem; as he used coal he had, of course, less need for wood, but the fact that a mechanical jack was used for cooking in the kitchen suggests that wood was certainly used for that. Three chimneys we know to have been swept every year – for kitchen, parlour and study and probably the chambers above these. My guess is that cooking was done on a wood fire and that the 'furnis' for heating water was coal-fuelled, as were the reception rooms and some bedrooms in winter. Coal in quantity was then measured in chaldrons (or 'chadrons' in the Accounts); thirty-six 'heaped' bushels then officially making a chaldron. A chaldron weighed rather more than one ton.

The Rector's coal probably came from mines in the north-east of the country, then moved by sea to London – hence the expression 'sea-coal' – and thence by barge to Streatley in exactly the same way as did his wine. From there it was moved by horse and cart to Lockinge, and a very laborious journey this must have been on the country roads of those days. Readers with local knowledge will probably know that there was then no road up Bull Hill at Streatley – it would, anyway, have been too steep for cartloads of coal – and that the journey was by way of East Ilsey. With little variation the Rector ordered five chaldrons of coal each year in May and paid out costs which break down roughly as follows:

5 chaldrons delivered to Streatley at 27*s*. a chaldron	£ 6. 15*s*. 0*d*.
Mileage, lighterage, carriage and wharphage	2. 15*s*. 10*d*.
Hire of 5 horses & carts to lift coal to Lockinge	2. 0*s*. 0*d*.
	£11. 10*s*. 10*d*.

Apart from enjoying those '-age' endings, one notes that the carriage and handling of the coal cost little less than the fuel itself. These charges varied from year to year, though not greatly. Mr

Aldworth on several occasions measures the number of bushels of coal making the chaldron that he received; they varied slightly from thirty-nine bushels to the chaldron to forty or forty-one: perhaps it depended how well the heaping was done. The Rector is, of course, careful to get the coal into the Rectory before haymaking should begin; indeed, in 1721, it was touch and go, the coal being collected on Monday the 19th of June and haymaking starting the day after. He always hired horses to carry the coal but the number varied – sometimes (as in the example quoted above) he hired all the transport needed; on other occasions, e.g. 1716, he hired only two teams, using four of his own. The teams would probably have moved via Blewbury and Harwell. The Rector himself went with them on at least one occasion, and in 1723 he spent five shillings at Streatley 'among the teams'.

To return now to the question raised earlier, the Rectory would have required wood fuel as well as the coal consumed at the rate of over six tons a year. The wood was necessary for cooking before the jack and for baking bread; it is not possible, unfortunately, to say how much wood he needed for this. Each February or March, two of the Rector's men cut and then stored the necessary faggots; Richard Day and John Edmunds usually made up the team and spent from eight to sixteen working days on this annual task. The source of this cut wood is not known, though faggotting was often combined with hedging so it must have been nearby. In 1723, for unknown reasons, Aldworth had to buy faggots from his farmer neighbour, William Smith, and they cost him 6*d.* a score, thus paying 5*s.* 7½*d.* for 225 of them. Then again in 1727 and 1728, he paid 14*s.* for 100 faggots no less than four times, nearly six times the previous price. I can find no explanation for this.

Appendix 5

LIST OF FOODSTUFFS MENTIONED IN THE ACCOUNT BOOKS
(Original spelling)

Fruit	*Item and cost where known*	*Notes*
Apples: red streak, pipin, pairmain		Tythable in kind
Apricots		Yearly gift from Farmer Hobbs
Cherries	1*s*. for 3lb	
*Currance	6*d*. a lb	
*Figs	4*d*. a lb	
Goosberrys		
Hops	6*d*.–1*s*. a lb	Tythable: subject to duty
*Lemmonds		
Mulberrys		Gift
*Oringes		
Pears		
Plumbs		
Quinces		Gift
*Raisins of the sun	5*d*. a lb	*N.B. *signifies not local*

Vegetables		
Artichooks or artichoques		
Cabbidge		
Colliflower		
Carrets		
Celery seed		
Colworts		Home grown
Cucumber	Once costed at 9*d*. for 150	Probably a gift
Ginee or guiny beans		
Greens		
Lettice		
Malagas	$3\frac{1}{2}$*d*.–4*d*. a lb	
Oinions	3 ropes for 8*d*.	
Peas	6*d*.–9*d*. a peck or gawne	
Radishes		
Roots		
Turnip seed		

Poultry		
Chickens	6*d*.–10*d*.	*General note*: These are probably live bird prices as the Rector kept his own poultry.
Ducks	2 for 1*s*. 6*d*.	
Geese	2*s*.–2*s*. 6*d*. e.	
Turkeys	2*s*. 6*d*.–3*s*. 6*d*. each	

Fish		
Anchoves		*General note*: Excludes local fish (see local game). In 1725 fish was brought from Ilsley and from Titchfield.
Crab	9*d*. or 10*d*. e.	
Lobster	1*s*. each	
Mackerill	6*d*. each	
Oysters	3*s*. 6*d*. a barrel	
Prawns		
Salt fish		
Shrimps		
Sturgeon		

Beverages other than wine		
Chocolate	10*s*. 6*d*. for an unknown quantity	
Cider	6 quarts for 1*s*.	
Coffee	About 4*s*. a lb	In 1721 a note reads: 'The first ½ of green coffee after it was roasted weighed 6 oz ½. This ½ pd of green coffee coud weigh but 7 oz: for the other weighed 9'
Tea		

Local Game		
Dotterill		Brought to the Rectory by locals and 6*d*. usually paid. A lerk is, of course, a lark.
Hare		
Lerks		
Partridge		
Pigeon		
Rabbits		
Quail		
Woodcock		

Fish

Eels		
Ling		
Par		Trout were frequently brought
Trout		to the house.

Other foodstuffs

Bread	1*d.* and 6*d.* loaves	
Butter	6*d.* a lb	
Cakes	2 for 6*d.*	
Candid oringe peel	1*s.* for ½lb	
Cheese	5*d.* a lb	
Cheddar cheese	6*d.* a lb	
Cream	3*d.* a pint	
Honey	3½*d.* a lb	50lb bought once.
Lard	4*d.* a lb	
Milk		
Oatmeale		
Rice		
Salt	£1 a sack	For salting meat: not table salt
Trecle		

Appendix 6

HOUSEHOLD AND OTHER OBJECTS MENTIONED IN THE ACCOUNTS

(Cost given when this is possible)

Household

Basket *4d.* Flag basket *7d.* or *8d.*
Bed curtains £1
Bed tick 12*s.* 6*d.*
Bellows 1*s.*
Besom 1*d.* Brew besom 6*d.*
Boyler £1. 18*s.* 0*d.*
Broom 6 for 7½*d.* Cane broom Flag broom 4*d.*
Stable broom 1*d.*
Brush 3*d.* Long brush 7*d.*
Bucket
Candles (Home-moulded) Watch candles 11*s.* 6*d.* for 2 doz.
Wax candles about 6*d.* per lb
Chaffing dish 1*s.* 6*d.* and 2*s.* 3*d.*
Chamberpots
Cloths Meat or cheese cloth 1*s.* each
Crockery
Earthenware
Forks
Glasses
Hoops (for tubs etc.) 2*d.*–4*d.* each
Knives
Lock for barn door 2*s.* 4*d.*
Mops 2½*d.* to 10*d.* each
Needles
Net 1*d.*
Paile Hand paile 1*s.*
Pans Milk pan frying pan
Pins
Plates Cheese plate waiting plate
Pots Tin pot 2*d.*
Rake 3½*d.*
Rush lights 2 dozen for 13*s.* 7lb for 7*s.*

Snuffer 10*d.*
Table Round cheese table 2*s.*
Tubbs Coal tubb wash tubb 10*s.* vinegar tubb 1*s.* 4*d.*
limbeck tubb 5*s.*

Miscellaneous

Corks 10*d.*–1*s.* 3*d.* per gross 45*s.*–50*s.* for 56lb
Brimstone
Flax 10*d.* a lb for tablecloths
Fuller's earth
Gunpowder & shot
Hemp
News sheets 1½*d.* each
Oil 3*s.* 3*d.* a bottle for spinning wool
Pattens 11*d.* a pair
Putty
Rabbit skins 2 for 1*s.*
Rennet 1*s.* 1*d.* a bag
Size
Sope 5*s.* a dozen 5*d.*–6*d.* a lb
Starch 5*d.* a lb

Firewood

2 cords (1 elm, 1 ash) cost £2. Very seldom bought.

CHAPTER FIVE

The charitable Rector

IT is worth mentioning at the start of this chapter that parish meetings (not necessarily connected with charity) were regular events and at these the Rector took a leading part. Documents of importance to the villagers were carefully kept in the 'Booke with green strings' as suggested by two entries in Aldworth's *aides-mémoire*. The first, in 1718, concerns William Moulden's certificate which was delivered by the Rector 'into the parishioners at their meeting on Easter Monday.' No further details are known. In 1723, Thomas Smith's Indenture was 'put in the Booke with green strings whence I took it.'

There had been a statutory requirement since 1601 for all parishes to provide relief for their own destitute. All landholders paid a tax (the Rector's contribution was £1 14*s*. 0*d*. a year) proportionate to their holdings. For actual detail we have to be satisfied by the few examples which John Aldworth elected to note down in his *aide-mémoire* and these follow. At least one can say that 'charity' was officially administered by people who knew each case intimately and who would have an interest in the person or family remaining usefully in the village.

One method, to take the pressure off a poor and overcrowded home, was to put one child (or more) into a more prosperous home as a temporary measure and to reimburse the hosts concerned – rather than pay money to the sufferer. Thus the Chair family parted with two of their sons; the elder went to William Smith and was clothed at parish expense: the younger went to Thomas Hobbs who was paid 6*d*. a week for the boy's board. Both hosts were farmers of some substance who also had young children of their own. A different approach was used where actual lack of housing happened; we do not know why Widow Yates and Goody Bozier were homeless but a Parish Meeting in 1722 accepted the offer of three farmers to 'set out some ground in Ginge whereon to build a house . . . at the Parish charge.' Unfortunately the outcome was not recorded. Only one example is given of an official grant of a weekly sum, with strings attached, and that concerned Ellen Green. She was given 18*d.* a week on the strict understanding that 'she kept herself clean and did not wander.' This condition proved too much for her and some weeks later the Rector noted that a Parish Meeting agreed she should be 'taken off the Poor Tax for her wandering.' Perhaps the poor old woman simply wandered out of the parish and out of touch.

One may say that John Aldworth, who was so seldom away from his parish, played a proper part in this official action against destitution: after all, it was in the interest of all those who employed labour that families continued to be solvent and therefore useful. His expenditure on 'Charity' is neatly set out each year under the heading 'Donations' and it is appropriate at this point to remind readers that the annual family income of labourers was estimated by Gregory King (in a famous survey of the class structure of England in 1688) at £15 a year – a figure I have found to be fairly accurate for Lockinge. Within such an income there would be very little room for saving against any kind of misfortune; a single visit by a doctor could cost the value of five days' labour.

It is quite possible to deduce John Aldworth's principles in helping others with money: briefly, the Rector's charity began at home but continued into his whole parish and beyond. His own household of servants and taskers was given special attention more in terms of gratitude and reward than of 'giving to the poor'; as well as the benefits already described, Aldworth usually gave each one 2*s.* 6*d.* on the great feast days, and after a spell of gout he would give each maid 5*s.* for her extra work. His next priority might properly be termed the deserving poor; such persons who attended the Sacrament on those same feast days would also receive 2*s.* 6*d.* – both poverty and religious observation being the required qualifications. Then there were those who fell into temporary difficulty, such as William Moulden when he broke his leg, and others who suffered from ague or smallpox and thus were off work for long periods. Smallpox never reached plague proportions between 1716 and 1729 but there were occasional small outbreaks in the village;

in 1723 two people died of it. In the case of Frank Church – of whom more will be heard – he had to leave school on the 8th of February 1717/18 on account of the smallpox and was not fit to return until the 5th of May.

There are many other examples of his kindliness which sometimes came in the form of sacks of wheat rather than money. I will cite a typical example, concerning the Noke family. John Noke was a labourer, not employed by the Rector, though his wife Mary was, living in his cottage with a garden but owning no other land. By 1716 the couple would probably have been in their forties; by 1721 Mary had given birth to twelve children – not a typical Lockinge family – of whom two had died young, leaving seven boys and three girls; up to this time, the only evidence of this family comes from the Parish Register, from the Rector's regular gifts to them at feast day Sacraments and his payment of two doctor's bills when John Noke fell ill. In 1721, Mary Noke felt able to leave her younger children in the care of her second daughter, Ann, then aged twelve, while she started casual work at the Rectory – the rough work of scouring, washing and weeding the garden. By then, however, yet another child had been conceived, her last as it turned out, and Mary stopped work exactly a fortnight before her son James was born. After an absence from work of some eight weeks, she resumed her job at the Rectory and indeed increased it, relying again on the faithful Ann, now aged fourteen years. In 1723 Ann and another of the Nokes' older children became seriously ill, probably with smallpox. John Aldworth paid for the doctor's bills but William, Ann's eldest brother, died. During and after these disasters, Mary Noke continued to work for the Rector until the time of his death, earning herself no more than £2 a year. Twice more the Rector paid a guinea for Mr Lockton or Mr Towsy, from Wantage, to visit the Nokes.

John Noke died in 1737, surviving his wife and leaving a will – unusual for a labourer – which deserves a note. Perhaps, in his ignorance, Noke omitted to appoint an executor to his will and though this legal flaw was overcome, it caused problems with probate. Having secured his goods, which were few, and the life tenure of his home, to his wife, he then left the north half of his house with half the backside and half the garden to one son and the south half of all this, together with a cowcommon, to another son. The outcome of this strange arrangement is not known, but the Noke family aptly illustrates the Rector's care of the poor. The Nokes were by no means the only ones.

A particular interest of John Aldworth was the education of certain village boys. There was, of course, no organised education at that time and such schools as existed were scarce; though there is no direct evidence of local schools or writing masters, both must have been in the vicinity, possibly at Wantage, as John Aldworth paid for a number of boys to attend both. Fees paid by the Rector varied from six shillings a year for the writing master – writing was then considered a quite separate study from reading – to two or four pence a week, possibly at a local dame's school, and up to ten shillings a quarter for a larger establishment. It is quite possible that John Aldworth was not the only wealthier inhabitant of Lockinge to send children to school, and no doubt some sent their own children. Aldworth's two godsons of his old age – there may have been earlier ones – received such benefits; they were Willy and Tom Smith, of different but connected local families, neither being in any sense poor. Each child was given generous presents, a silver spoon for Willy at his Christening, and 9*s*. 6*d*. for Tom. When Will Smith (one of at least four living William Smiths) was ten and a half years old, the Rector notes down: 'I advised Mrs Smith to send Will to writing: promised to pay the writing master.' This duly started the following January and continued for several years. Tom Smith was sent off to school at a much younger age, five and a half, and continued there at the Rector's expense until the death of the latter when Tom was nine years old. Less well-to-do parents were also helped with the education of a boy; William, son of Richard Day, went to school at the Rector's expense for three years and Jonathan Atkins, son of John Aldworth's faithful servant, also. It is as well to remember that parents had a difficult choice between education and the necessity for a boy to start learning a trade and earning some money – which could start even at the age of twelve. At the other end of the social scale, Aldworth helped with the education costs of a cousin called Withrington, paying no less than two guineas a year. One senses a certain distaste: 'Withrington' is never accorded a Christian name and the Rector's last entry is, to say the least, snappish, being only a month or so before his death:

'30 Jun 1729. To Cousin Withrington (He should not have come till July) £2. 12. 6'

John Aldworth's greatest kindness in the field of educating young Lockinge boys in the last years of his life was the case of Frank Church. Why he chose one of the Church family of eight children is not known. Indeed the Lockinge Parish Register does not show a Francis Church among this family which consisted of Thomas and Mary and, on the face of it, their four boys and four girls, all born between 1694 and 1710. Thomas Church's wife died in 1713 and it is probable that he married again as the Easter Offering shows both husband and wife up to the year 1722 when all mention of them ceases. Thomas Church was a Lockinge man holding a little land and a flock of sheep; in 1718 he provided the Rector with a horse for the carriage of Rectory grain to corn-merchants on no less than sixteen occasions, but he neither worked for the Rector nor otherwise did business with him. The facts in John Aldworth's Accounts suggest decline and eventual departure, perhaps to do better elsewhere. One might therefore be doubtful about the origins of Frank Church, but luckily the Public Record Office hold Apprentice Books for the period – Frank was eventually to become an apprentice – which show him as the son of Thomas Church of East Lockinge, Berkshire. His omission from the Parish Register could have several explanations, including forgetfulness on the part of the Rector.

Frank was about thirteen years old in 1716 and had probably been under the Rector's care before that; from then onwards he is mentioned repeatedly in the Accounts. Firstly, he went to school at the Rector's expense, at a cost of ten shillings a quarter, paid to a Mr Barton. Then a writing master was also employed and the Rector not only paid for him but for a number of books: *Aesop's Fables*, a Latin Testament and a Greek one. Finally, John Aldworth paid for all the boy's clothes and shoes during the year. These included Thomas Kimber making up a frock, waistcoat and breeches (for 5*s*.); knitted stockings, a pair of gloves; no less than four pairs of shoes (3*s*. a pair, 3*s*. 4*d*. with nails) and two pairs mended. This suggests a good deal of walking by Frank Church, and my guess is that the clothes provided were a form of school uniform and the walking was to and from Wantage to school each week-day. In 1717 the process continued, the books provided this year being a Lexicon, a Gradus (a Latin or Greek dictionary) and a book of Horace – all this suggesting the normal classical education of a gentleman. However, in November of that year, comes a surprising entry:

'21 Nov. pd Nn Absolom for cleaning Fr Church from Lice 2*s*6*d*'

On Saturday the 14th of December, Frank's school broke up for Christmas, re-opening on Monday the 13th of January. Three weeks later, Frank had to be removed, suffering from smallpox, and was seriously ill, requiring several visits from Mr Lockton. But, encouraged by his patron's generosity ('2*s* before Frank had smallpox, 2*s* 6*d* after it came out.') he slowly recovered and was able to return to school in early May. He did not stay there long. John Aldworth had arranged for him to be apprenticed to a London clockmaker, Mr Daniel Kedden, at his own expense, and Frank went off to London by carriage, on the 21st of July 1718, where he was formally apprenticed to Kedden for seven years on the 7th of July. The clockmaker was paid £20 for taking the boy on and 10*s*. duty was paid to the Government – all from the pocket of the Rector of East Lockinge. Nor did his kindness to Frank Church end there. He sent £3 twice a year to Mr Kedden to pay for the boy's clothes until 1724, when a curious entry occurs in the Accounts:

'20 May. To Mr Kedden bound for a son 23*s*.'

which might be taken to mean that Mr Kedden had formally adopted Frank. The year before, young Church had returned to Lockinge – one hopes that he came to thank John Aldworth – and the latter noted in his Accounts that his protegé had then completed five years of his apprenticeship. That is the last we hear of Frank Church – and it is fair to add that John Aldworth had laid out just under £70 in those seven years between 1716 and 1723 in order to launch a village boy on a promising career; he must have had great confidence in him.

A last illustration of the Rector's kindness to the poorer labourers of the parish is now given, showing his preference for giving in kind rather than in cash. Among his tithe receipts was a due of one fleece for every ten sheep wintered in the parish, a tithe which he took in kind. 1724 was in fact a peak year for Lockinge sheep with over 1,100 of them wintering, and 106 fleeces were therefore set aside for the Rector at shearing time. John Aldworth then decided to use some of this wool (admittedly the 'coarser wool') for the benefit of twelve parishioners instead of his usual sale of the wool on the open market. The detail of this is now given in the form of the sequence of the events concerned:

		£	s.	d.
1.	**The raw material**			
	102lb of the coarser wool was set aside,			
	valued at 5*d.* per lb	£2	2*s.*	6*d.*
2.	**Spinning**			
	The wool was spun in two lots, one of 38lb			
	Cost of spinning		16*s.*	0*d.*
	The other lot of 61lb was spun at a cost of	£1	5*s.*	5*d.*
	The necessary oil cost		8*s.*	1½*d.*
	Total cost of spinning	£2	9*s.*	6½*d.*
3.	**Milling, weaving and scouring** by the weaver, Mr Brown			
	The 38lb of spun wool was woven into 23 yards of cloth			
	at a cost of		19*s.*	0*d.*
	The 61lb of spun wool was woven into 32 yards of cloth			
	at a cost of	£1	6*s.*	8*d.*
	Scouring cost		1*s.*	6*d.*
	Total cost of weaving	£2	7*s.*	2*d.*
4.	**Making up the cloth** by Thomas Kimber, the tailor			
	From 23 yards of cloth, he made 3 coats. With buttons etc.			
	at a cost of		14*s.*	9*d.*
	and also one coat and two waistcoats. With buttons etc.			
	at a cost of		9*s.*	6*d.*
	From 32 yards of cloth, he made 7 coats. With buttons etc.			
	at a cost of	£1	15*s.*	6*d.*
	Total cost of making up	£2	19*s.*	9*d.*
	Total cost of ten coats and two waistcoats, including value of wool	£9	18*s.*	11½*d.*

The coats were given to ten named men, all married parishioners of various ages, the only common factor being poverty. A waistcoat went to the son of two of the chosen men. Of them all, only two had a direct connection with the Rectory: Jonathan Atkins, Aldworth's leading tasker and former servant, and John Noke, whose wife, as we know, worked at the Rectory. The figures are also of interest as they show the probable cost of a coat to an ordinary labourer, if he had to buy one. The cost would have been about eighteen shillings, no less than the value of eighteen days of his labour.

Outside the parish, the Rector met an extraordinarily varied number of cries for help. Firstly there were the briefs circulated to parishes from all over the country calling for subscriptions to mitigate some natural disaster, the commonest being fire or flood. Each had to be read from the pulpit and the Rector, in his Accounts, naturally only enters his own contribution. Many briefs were for churches, often struck by lightning, followed by fire. Examples were 'Oxtead Church Surry Burnt by Lightning' and another unnamed building in Staffordshire which, as recorded by Aldworth, was damaged 'by thunder' to the value of £4,163 in necessary repairs. Other briefs affected communities such as a small village in Sussex, now called Brighton; '3 Feb 1722. To Brighthelmston in Sussex lost by overflowing of the sea – £8000.' There were a steady eight to twelve briefs dealt with every year and few could have been more surprising to the Lockinge congregation than their Rector's call one year to support the Episcipalian Churches of Poland and Transylvania. John Aldworth, who normally gave a shilling or so to each brief, produced no less than a pound for this appeal – possibly, one might guess, for lack of village support.

There were many vagrants who called at the Rectory, and if evidence is needed that Lockinge lay close to a main east-west route, Aldworth's kindness to such passers-by gave proof. Quite a number were sailors or soldiers, almost all carried a pass of authenticity; others had been shipwrecked and were on their way to their homes. There were foreigners – Turks, Arabs and Spaniards – and each was helped on his way by the kind old Rector of Lockinge. 'Fandy, a Turk become a Christian' certainly knocked on the right door, receiving five shillings: the journeys of some were long – from Ipswich to Bristol; Exeter to Oxford; Minehead to Harwich; Southampton to Lincoln. One example shows not only the perils of shipwreck but of a very long walk home when you had lost all your belongings:

'11 Nov 1717. To a Gentleman of Bellew Lincolnshire His ship founderd at sea but he set ashore at Minehead – 1 shilling.'
The Rector's compassion was not, however, blind – as shown in the case of 'one of faringdon pretending a Los by fire more than he suffered He reckoning the House wch was not his.' This suggests astute questioning before charity flowed, but the man got his shilling. Fire was a very frequent cause of destitution and every year John Aldworth helped one or more sufferers. 1721 was a particularly bad year in those parts for fire damage and the dates below suggest that the culprit was a hot, dry summer:

29 Jul To Wernom of Chivly, Burnt down	1*s*
4 Aug To 2 Drayton men, Los by fire £300	2*s*
26 Sep or before. To Atwell 2*s* A maid 1*s* Winterborne all of Wantage & sufferers by fire	5*s*
5 Oct To Henry Allen of Hanny losing £50 by fire	1*s*

All the places mentioned are fairly near to Lockinge.

There are also entries which catch the eye, such as a gift of five shillings to the son of Archbishop Sancroft's sister – a very unlikely vagrant – and a local Harwell man who had been robbed on Hounslow Heath of fifteen guineas. For sheer persistence by the one, and true compassion by the other, the following entries tell their own story:

18 Sep 1723 To Baker Stait's wife	1*s*
3 Apr 1724 To Stait's wife of Wantage promising never to come again	1*s*
13 Mar 1726 To Mrs Stait of Wantage she promises as once before not to come again	1*s*.

I have given only a few examples of John Aldworth's kindly actions to others in distress. As will follow in this story, the Rector's will completed his charitable acts and, though there is no evidence of it in the Accounts, *The History of the Parish of East Lockinge* quotes yet another charity :

'The Rev J Aldworth, Rector, left £6 to the deserving poor and £2 towards the stipend of the Parish Clerk, annually.'
This is curious as there is no mention of this in his will.

CHAPTER SIX

The farming Rector: arable crops

BEFORE going into the detail of John Aldworth's grain crops, which provided more than half his income, it is proper to set Lockinge in a wider context of farming as then practised in the south of England. To do this, I have consulted *The Agrarian History of England*, edited by Joan Thirsk (1984), for the period 1640–1750, as well as M.A.Havinden's *Estate Villages* which is particularly concerned with the Lockinge area.

From this reading, it is evident that Lockinge was entirely typical of the local pattern of sheep and corn country, as opposed to the dairy farming areas in the Vale of the White Horse. This was because of its strip-like parish area, reaching from well-watered meadows in the north, up through chalkland to the Downs in the south. Lockinge also then conformed to the open-field, small-scale farming units then to be found in those parts. The village economy was based on a small number of 500-acre tenant farmers and a large number of smaller holders of land, all tenants of absentee landlords. All this was to change very soon after Aldworth's death in 1729, when one landlord began to make larger farming units on his land. The older method, though less efficient, made for a remarkably self-sufficient community, with grain surpluses sufficient to sell to corn-dealers. Wheat and barley from the Home Counties were then in increasing demand to feed a growing London and it is noticeable that the buyers of Aldworth's grain were generally in the area east of Lockinge and towards the River Thames, carrying grain in bulk by barge to the capital – by far the most economical way of doing it. Grain prices then were directly related to demand, lean harvests leading to high prices; and within each year, prices tended to rise as time went by and stocks lowered. Thus the fetching price of grain varied from year to year and from month to month.

The Agrarian History of England gives average prices which pertained in the south of England for each decade of that period and these do correspond fairly closely with the prices obtained by John Aldworth. I can only make a comparison between seven years of his farming (1720–6) with ten years (1720–9) of average prices in the southern counties of England, but I think these figures are worth including. They are given in shillings per quarter, bearing in mind that the figures for Aldworth's grain are for only 443 quarters (wheat) and 727 quarters (barley):

	Wheat	*Barley*
South of England average price	33.99	19.65
Aldworth's average price	32.37	20.50

Wool production in Berkshire is known to have been declining even before John Aldworth's time and this is born out in Lockinge Parish by the relatively small flocks of sheep wintering there, each of some 200 sheep, owned by five or six of the larger farmers. The Rector had no need to keep sheep himself as he received one tenth of the fleeces shorn every year in tithes. He, like his fellow farmers, then sold his wool in the markets of Reading, Newbury or Abingdon which, though not as important as before, still manufactured shalloon, sacking and sail-cloth.

In simplified summary, Lockinge fits in very closely to the description of farming in that area found in *The Agrarian History of England.* It could be said that the Rector, through his servant and farm bailiff, Rob Absolom, relied on his grain crops to produce much of his income and on his livestock to make his operations more or less self-sufficient in transport and food. But this is not the whole picture.

So far little mention has been made of another strong bond between John Aldworth and his parishioners. Not only was his flock a mere two hundred or so souls, virtually all committed members of his church, but he was engaged in exactly the same way of earning a living as they were.

Every man, woman and child in Lockinge depended on farming in one way or another and the Rector was no exception; he intimately understood their problems by sharing in them; he bought and sold among them and he employed a few of them. Granted a good man – and John Aldworth, I think, qualifies – there can seldom have been a closer or a more understanding relationship between priest and flock than that of Lockinge in those days.

As admitted earlier, there is no direct evidence today either of the size of the Rector's glebe or its location in the village; the only enclosed piece of glebe about which I am reasonably sure is Barton Close. Then it was simply part of the glebe land; later it was to become the site of a new Rectory which stands today. Using very indirect methods, such as comparing his average crop yield with an average per acre in those days, the whole glebe might have been perhaps 75–100 acres in all and a good deal of it lay within the common fields. This we know from his descriptions of where crops were sown.

Readers may remember that John Aldworth's surviving Account Books include considerable detail from 1716 to 1729 but that only Yearly Book Summaries survive for the earlier years from 1685. These simply show the sum totals of each Account Heading.

In the case of the Year Books, we are dealing with statistics unsupported by any sort of detail or comment and must therefore be most cautious in any conclusions drawn. The figures below cover the years from 1686 to 1726, 1685 being incomplete and 1727–9 somewhat unreliable. The Rector recorded sums of money to the farthing – I shall round them off to the nearest pound sterling:

	Total	*Yearly average*
Total tithe & farm receipts	£12,874	£314
Farm expenses	3,461	84
Thus the clear profit	9,413	230
Other expenses	8,445	206
Thus the overall saving	968	24

These figures surely show the need for detailed account keeping. Mr Micawber was not the first to discover that only a small swing from profit to loss leads from happiness to misery. John Aldworth in fact recorded an overall deficit (or as he says 'ran out') in only thirteen of the forty-one years. The second interesting fact is the low level of farm expense compared with receipt, his expenses being on average just over a quarter of his receipts. A clear profit was an annual certainty and was usually above £200. Some readers may wish to see the annual variation within these figures and these are given in the form of a graph at Appendix 7. They will see from it that grain prices (which are the basis of farm receipts) seem to peak every twelve or thirteen years, as is suggested in *The Agrarian History of England*; the high peaks on the graph in 1697 and 1709 mark years of widespread harvest failure, causing high grain prices. The graph also shows that the Rector was at no time in debt; a study of his accumulated overall profits shows a steady growth, allowing him to ride heavy items of capital expenditure, such as a repair bill in 1698 to his buildings of over £170.

A breakdown of the average farm receipt figures (£314) in the Year Books shows the following:

	Per year
Wheat	£107
Barley	98
Hay	45
Oats, beans & peas	38
Other sources:	
(petty tithes, straw & chaff)	26

The wheat harvest for 1697 – we do not know the quantity sold, only its value – was worth no less than £236.

Coming now to the period 1716–26, for which full and reliable details are available, I propose to discuss a few points which relate to all those years and then to concentrate on one particular year, 1718, in which we can follow the farm calendar, the work done, the men and women who did it, and what they were paid.

Firstly, then, a look at the Rector's crops over those ten or so years. We can now see the prices fetched for the Rector's crops, and it is at once noticeable that they vary not only from year to year but also from month to month, usually rising to a peak in midwinter when stocks might be running low. These variations within a year are not very great; most years started with a wheat price of about 3*s*. 6*d*. a bushel rising to perhaps 4*s*. in winter and falling back to 3*s*. 6*d*. later; in 1725, however, the opening price was 5*s*. 6*d*. rising in February to 6*s*. 6*d*. Barley, being almost entirely sold in bulk, was always priced by the quarter (there being eight bushels to a quarter) and the price of it also varied; in 1720 the price opened at 24*s*. 6*d*. a quarter, while in 1722 it stood at 14*s*. 6*d*. a quarter for most of the year; the names of buyers and some of their locations are known. What is noticeable is that there are a lot of them, the Rector having dealings with no less than thirty-seven different buyers over the ten years, in disposing of his wheat and barley. This rather suggests that the grain was sold by sample at market and then delivered to the buyers who came from villages such as Streatley, Chilton, West Ilsley, Hagbourne, Harwell, Aston Tirrold and South Moreton, as well as Newbury. That this was the case is suggested by an Account entry recording a sale of barley to Jonathan Acres in 1720. After the price, the comment 'hard and fast' is added, indicating, I think, that there could be no bargaining.

Haymaking and harvest did not, of course, start on fixed dates but, generally, haymaking started in the latter half of June and finished in late July or early August. Harvesting, however, always started the next working day and ran to about mid-September. 1723 was a difficult year for farmers, with just a fortnight's haymaking in the first two weeks of July, followed at once by a harvest which went on for eight weeks, and indeed beyond, the last entry being: '25 Oct. We ended Harvest by a load of Barley from Ginge.' Only once is seed wheat identified – White Lammas. Whereas most of his barley is sold to dealers, John Aldworth often sold small quantities of a bushel or two of wheat to parishioners, sometimes making a gift of it to needy ones. What must have been inferior grain – its price is lower – is referred to either as 'parings of the front' or as 'brickt wheat'. Crops suffered from smut in several years.

A last matter before moving to a particular year. I have been interested to find out the extent to which 'cash flow' affected a farmer of those times, bearing in mind that his largest wages bills were in the spring and summer while payment for his crops did not come until autumn and winter. Taskers, daily paid men, with few if any savings, had their lean months in the late winter. I conclude that, in effect, farmers – and particularly farming Rectors – acted as local banks. With their resources, they could stand a cash outflow and would lend money to those who needed tiding over – an example being the harvesters who were not paid until it was completed: another is the Rector's hired servants who were paid annually in arrears. Such loans are carefully recorded in John Aldworth's Accounts. The extent to which the Rector needed a reserve of money is apparent from studying the ebb and flow of his cash month by month. In 1717, for example, Aldworth paid out over £73 more than he received in the months from April to August: thereafter the position is reversed and, over the rest of the year to March, he is in pocket to some £50. This was a year when he made a small overall loss.

And now for 1718, chosen for the good reason that the names and acreages of all the tenant farmers in Lockinge – with the one exception of the Rector – are known from a levy, based on land tenure, to repair the church. For this I am indebted to M.A.Havinden's book *Estate Villages*.

King George I was on the throne, the first Jacobite rebellion had been put down, and relative peace established in Europe by means of the Triple Alliance of England, France and Holland. A Whig government was in power and likely to stay so, having passed the Septennial Act in 1716. In East Lockinge, the levy for repairing the church – which raised just over £3. 5*s*. 0*d*. – shows thirty-five tenants of land, totalling some 130 yardlands, or about 3,900 acres. Taking an arbitrary figure of 100 acres as the top limit of a smallholder, there are twenty-five of these. The top five farmers – those farming over 400 acres – were Thomas Hobbs (560 acres), Mr Charles Collins (510 acres), Farmer Reading, a bachelor newcomer (495) acres, Farmer Munt (425 acres) and William Smith (420 acres). They are at once recognisable in the Easter Offering by their paying for their servants, and on the Downs by their flocks of sheep. The first sign of a considerable change approaching Lockinge is the departure of Mr Prouze, the lord of the manor:

'27 May. Robert corded up Mr. Prouze his Trunke & Mr. Knapp's Bond cancelled was naild upon it, with 6 nails, for a Direction. I showd the bond cancelld to my sister & Rob before it was naild on.'

Something is known about these farmers. Charles Collins, in particular, would have been a friend of the Rector. The former, a younger man than John Aldworth (he was aged fifty-two in 1718, his Rector sixty-six) came of a family accustomed, like the Aldworths, to sending their sons up to Oxford, in their case to Pembroke College, where they claimed Founder's Kin, before studying the law or taking holy orders. During his incumbency John Aldworth had baptised no less than ten of Charles' children – he was widowed three times – and buried six of those ten. Both men were Commissioners of the Land Tax for many years and worked together on the Parish Charity and Vestry Meetings.

Very little is known, however, of Farmer Thomas Reading who did not come from a local family; he had replaced the Castles as tenants of West Ginge, but left the tenancy by 1722. William Munt was an older man whose wife had died the previous year (1717). He then had grown-up children, farmed at West Ginge and survived John Aldworth's death in 1729. William Smith came from such a mass of Smiths baptised at Lockinge that even the Rector has difficulty in telling one from another; this one was dubbed 'William the elder' or 'Long William' and he lived at a house called Alleblasters, the only house, except Betterton, named in the Accounts. Lastly, there was Thomas Hobbs, married to a local girl, Mary Bunce, in 1705, and having six young children – two more being born in 1719 and in 1722. Following him through the Accounts, one has the impression of a slow decline in his affairs. It may be remembered that he took in one of Dame Chair's boys, as an act of charity, in 1721, and there are many entries in the Accounts of his wife supplying the Rectory with butter, apricots and pears; in paying for one consignment, the Rector adds '. . . and for many other kindnesses'. But by 1722, no Hobbs servants are shown in the Easter Offering and in 1723, John Aldworth began to give the family 2*s*. 6*d*. a month under his heading of 'Charity' though we do not know its actual reason. Finally, all mention of the family ceased in 1725, so one must presume that they left the area.

Among the rest of the parishioners – there were about forty heads of families in 1718 – there was a descending order of smallholders, a small number of artisans who also held land, and finally a few who laboured only for others. This well-established order was to change later towards fewer, consolidated larger farms, a reduction of the number of smallholders and an increase of landless labourers. Actual 'Enclosure' with a capital E, authorised by Act of Parliament, was still a long way off, but Matthew Wymondsold was to make the changes described above, to build for himself a manor house by the church, surrounded by parkland, and to have the Rectory rebuilt elsewhere. This unpopular man's family had never lived locally, but he had speculated successfully with the South Sea Company and was sufficiently wealthy to buy the Manors of Ginge and Lockinge about 1720. One would expect much mention of this new Lord of the Manor in Aldworth's Accounts, but in fact there are very few; he does not appear in the Easter Offerings. He and his sons certainly came to live in Lockinge – there is a surviving painting of them there – but they had all gone by the end of the century. Readers who remember 'Burials in Woollen' mentioned earlier may be interested to know that Wymondsolds were not so buried, but that their coloured page boy was: 'Christopher Othello, negro servant of Mr Wymondsold, was buryed July 23, 1771, in woollen only.'

Early in 1718, the physician, Mr Lockton – probably of Wantage, he was not a Lockinge parishioner – had had to attend the Rector, his sister Susannah and also Frank Church for reasons unknown. The last-named went off to London as an apprentice in July of that year, as already recounted.

Turning now to the farm accounts, it is worth noting at the outset that Aldworth accounted all crops harvested in a year to belong to it, even if some of the crop was sold in the following year. For example, his 1718 wheat crop was still being sold in April, May and June of 1719 but was nevertheless within the 1718 accounts. In all other matters – sowing, threshing and winnowing – these were accounted for simply in the year in which they fell. In 1718, the wheat, beans and vetches crops had been sown the previous year in

October, November and March respectively (readers are again reminded of New Year's Day then being the 25th of March); only the barley and some more vetches were sown in April of 1718. The sowing was done by one of the hired men-servants or a tasker. John Aldworth uses several land measures which, I deduce from various clues, are related as follows: two halves make one land; one land is the same as an acre. Mentioned in the Church Levy, but not by Aldworth, was the yardland, which approximated to thirty acres. Having said this, I can now compare the sowing rates mentioned in *The Agrarian History of England* with those of the Rector – and here there is a marked difference:

	Bushels per acre	
	Wheat	*Barley*
Agrarian History of England	2¼	3¾
John Aldworth	1¼–1½	3–3½

In the year 1718, the Rector's total farm income, before deducting expenses was:

	Value	*% of total*
The sale of barley	£106	35·33
The sale of wheat	84	28
Tithe receipts	40	13·33
Other sources	70	23·33
	£300	

The subject of tithes will be dealt with later. It is worth mentioning in this chapter that tithes related to produce sold, thus the bulk of them were paid by the richer farmers. They came to the Rector in both cash and kind. Of the £40 above, the 'top five' farmers found just over half the money and goods.

The farming year opened with Jack Day ploughing before the vetches were sown in May. The Days were numerous in Lockinge, as has been said already; Richard and Mary Day worked for the Rector, the former full-time. Jack was their nephew, then aged fourteen, who earned 3*d.* a day for ploughing – whether unsupervised is not known – but, as his little brother was paid 2*d.* for leading the horses while Jack ploughed, (on another occasion), it seems as if Jack was in charge. The month of May often seemed the least busy, before the coming labours of haymaking and harvest. One activity persisted steadily – the threshing and winnowing of the 1717 crops which was only completed five days before haymaking started on Monday the 23rd of June.

In fact, Richard Day and John Edmunds had begun on it a week or so earlier and were joined by the two men-servants, Rob Absolom and Jonathan Atkins. The gathered hay was at once carried to a barn ('laid up in the House in my ground') ready for future use, chiefly in the stables, to the extent of 57 cocks. Hay is variously quantified in loads, parcels and cocks. Hay was not cheap and these 57 cocks were valued by the Rector at £7. 12*s.* 6*d.* As well as his own hay, Aldworth received hay in tythe, usually in money; in this particular year, he had a sufficient crop of hay to sell some to others. Under the heading of 'Hay', hop clover, ray grass and sinkfoile are mentioned in other years. An interesting fact emerges about the wages of the two haymaking men. They are each paid ninepence a day for this work, threepence less than the standard wage – which appears a strange injustice; but a note in the 1719 Accounts makes it clear that the full haymaking wage was abated by the value of their meals, taken in the Rectory. Including the value of each day's food and drink, they were in fact 2*d.* above the standard rate. The whole matter of wages will be discussed later.

Before early July, a most necessary and laborious preliminary to the harvest was in progress. Elizabeth Cullam, recently a grandmother and nearer fifty than forty in age, twice hoed five acres of beans and then weeded the wheat and barley crops. Field labour by women was paid then by the piece, not by the day, presumably to allow them to do the job when convenient provided it was done in time. Goody Cullam was paid as much as £1 for the hoeing and 5*s.* 9*d.* for the weeding. Although we do not know how long this took, the money represents over fifty days' labour at the standard woman's rate of 6*d.* a day.

The stage now being set and the labour force available, the

harvest work started on Monday the 21st of July. Absolom, Atkins, Edmunds and Day (all in fact referred to by their master by their Christian names) were joined by William Winterbourne at the end of the first week. William was by trade a carpenter and builder who held no land; he helped with the Rector's harvest practically every year and perhaps enjoyed the change. The wages of these three taskers are interesting: Winterbourne and Richard Day get 14*d.* a day, but John Edmunds only 12*d.* Further study of other harvests shows that in fact 14*d.* was the standard wage for a day's harvesting with meals provided as well; why Edmunds was paid but 12*d.* in 1718 is not known. In another year, 1723, he was paid the basic 14*d.* and because he was not fed by the Rectory, he received a further 7*d.* a day, making 1*s.* 9*d.* in all. While the men worked at the reaping, two women, Goody Edmunds (John's wife) and Goody Kimber (wife of the local tailor), were busy cocking two and a half acres of barley: soon after, Goody Day (Richard's wife) helped pick beans and then joined Goody Edmunds in helping to build a bean rick, which was duly thatched in August. The Accounts, of course, give no detail of the team method of reaping and cocking, nor of the carting.

Almost at once, preparations began for sowing next year's wheat. Several days dung-spreading, followed by the plough, led to the sowing of six and a half bushels of seed wheat (the Rector's own) on four and a half acres or lands in late October. Towards the end of the year, in February 1718/19, barley and beans were again sown, and yet another lot of beans in early March before the New Year.

All this work was done by one or more of the Rector's team, with the occasional help of an outsider for a day or two. It had to be fitted in with the threshing and winnowing and the despatch of grain to buyers.

Threshing was a man's job, usually worked at in pairs; winnowing was often done by a woman. In 1718, the threshing was mainly done by Richard Day who worked at the 1718 harvest for no less than thirty-seven long weeks with barely a break on other work. John Edmunds dealt with the previous year's crops until June but was replaced by Charles Cannon after the harvest during October,

November and December. The reasons are not known and the replacement was unusual – Day and Edmunds did the Rector's threshing every year except 1718, until Edmund's death in 1726. Then, through the autumn, as the new crops came in, a number of local smallholders came to the Rectory to thresh and to buy the resulting barley and bean straw for 3*s.* a day's threshing. If one thinks about it, this arrangement ingeniously suited everyone. The harder the buyer worked, the more straw he got for the fixed price of 3*s.*; meanwhile, the Rector had much of his barley and beans threshed without cost to himself. In 1718, this involved thirteen local men, including Rob Absolom and John Edmunds, on a total of some forty days. Wheat straw was separately dealt with, being sold locally at 3*d.* a dozen (whatever that may have meant) though, strangely, not to Richard Tame, the village thatcher. Readers may recall that in the previous year, the Rector and Rob Absolom had quarrelled over the loading of thirty dozen straw and that the argument turned on whether this was one cartload or two – which gives some idea of the bulk of thirty dozen of straw.

Winnowing was shared between the Rector's men-servants and Richard Day's wife; a few others helped occasionally. The rewards for winnowing were both small and difficult to determine in the case of task work; that done by the two men-servants was, of course, part of their annual salary. Goody Day is the principal winnower among the taskers and she earns sums of 3*d.* or 6*d.* which suggests a half-daily or daily rate respectively, 6*d.* being the standard woman's wage. Her son Jack sometimes joins her, in which case they earn 6*d.* between them; some idea of the yearly task of winnowing is apparent from the fact that, in 1718, a total of over 200 quarters or 1600 bushels were dealt with.

While this went on six days a week, Rob Absolom was often busy selling his master's grain. The distribution of it (for 1718) is of interest:

	Figures in quarters			
	Wheat	*Barley*	*Beans/peas*	*Oats*
Total crop	55	116	32	12
Sold locally in small amounts	15	None	7	None
A little sold to dealers in loads of 5qrs. or more	35	106	6	None
A little retained for home use	5	10	19	12

Home uses:
Wheat: used for the Rectory flour – a good deal of the 1717 wheat was also used for this. The 1718 crop provided seed wheat for 1719.
Barley: 9 quarters were sent to the miller for malting and then used for the Rectory brews. 1 quarter was used for pig and horse fodder.
Beans/peas: used as fodder for horses and pigs.
Oats: for horses. An extra 5 quarters had to be bought in 1718.

It seems that corn-dealers regarded delivery as part of the deal and the Rector had to use either his own or hired transport. 1718 was, in this respect, out of the run, as Aldworth, from December onwards, used horses hired from Thomas Church, the father of Frank, the apprentice; this happened no less than twelve times to deliver barley to Streatley, Ilsley and Hagbourne. Normally, John Aldworth only hired horses for his yearly consignments of coal and wine.

I have not mentioned any system of crop rotation because of the difficulty of identifying particular plots of land, but the evidence is that some sort of rotation was used.

Other work done by men on the Rector's land should be mentioned, even though this comes under the heading of 'Other Expenses' in his Accounts. Stone clearing was one – a laborious job, done not only to clear the land but also to discharge the landholder's duty to keep parish roads in some sort of repair. Hedging and ditching was another yearly chore, faggotting another and, from time to time, the stream which passed through the Rectory grounds had to be cleared. In the Rectory itself there was, of course, housework and washing to be done – much of it by village women – and in the garden, there was the planting and weeding.

It is not easy to assess the working life of the labourer in those days. People then worked a twelve-hour day, with short intervals for meals, every day of the year, except Sundays and Christmas Day, unless no work was obtainable. John Aldworth's Accounts offer rare evidence of this, showing the weekly amounts paid to each of his weekly-paid men. Not all of them work full-time for the Rector, but one or two did, so that we really can see just how many days they worked and what they earned for that work. When daylight shortened, the twelve-hour day was reduced to ten and the standard wage for a man dropped from one shilling to tenpence per day. A woman was paid sixpence a day and a boy threepence or fourpence. So slow was the change in rural England that it is appropriate to quote Mavor's *Survey of Berkshire* of 1809. As the author aptly remarks: 'In the edifice of human society, the common people are the grand base on which the superstructure of rank and property is reared.' In a later chapter, he concedes the price paid for this: 'Though the wages of agricultural labour are increased at least one fourth within the last ten years, they are still inadequate to support a family without driving a man, on every emergency, to the parish for assistance.' This last extract is certainly borne out by the Aldworth Account Books; whether they felt charitably inclined or not, the employers of farm labour would wish to keep their men fit for their strenuous work; and yet, as we have seen in an earlier chapter, John Aldworth's servants were not afraid of him. That fact is strong evidence of his genuine concern for his people.

Another generalised guide to wages comes from Gregory King's breakdown of the population of England, in 1688, into social classes, estimating the size of the family and its income in each case – obviously a very rough and ready estimate. He gave England's population then as five and a half million, of which just under half were reckoned to be in the following groups, given in descending order and including their families:

	Persons	Annual income per family
Labourers and outservants	1,275,000	£15. 0*s*. 0*d*.
Cottagers & paupers	1,300,000	£ 6. 10*s*. 0*d*.
Vagrants	30,000	—

Thanks to John Aldworth, the yearly family income for at least one labourer in Lockinge is known very precisely because both he and his wife worked continually for the Rector on wages which are recorded weekly in the Accounts. I count this as an important piece of evidence. As *The Agrarian History of England* (in Vol. V, pt. II, Chapter 13) states, concerning this period: 'The number of days on which wage earners worked in the course of a year is an unknown quantity.'

We shall shortly deal with the particular case of Richard Day and his family in 1718, but it is worth adding that Gregory estimated a 'gentleman's family' to enjoy £280 a year and 'a lesser clergyman' a mere £50 a year – by which reckoning, John Aldworth was more gentleman than minor clergy. Even 'eminent clergymen' do not rise above £72 a year.

In the year 1718, John Aldworth's chief worker was undoubtedly Richard Day. This man was one of a large tribe of Lockinge Days, all related to each other and often of the same Christian name; however, Richard may be identified as being aged thirty-four, with a wife named Mary, and one two year-old son, William; Mary also worked for the Rector, as did two nephews, Jack Day and Tom Day, aged fifteen and ten respectively in 1718.

Richard worked six days a week for almost all the year for the Rector and it is clear that, except for three days off at Christmas, he had no holidays; when he is off work, this is because the Rector has no work to give him. This happened on just thirty working days in the year – Richard worked on 280 days and rested on 52 Sundays and 3 weekdays over Christmas. For this he received £13 13*s*. 7*d*. In broad terms, he spent most of the year threshing, except for June, July and August, when he was part of the haymaking and harvesting team. Otherwise he did a number of jobs: cleaving wood, faggotting, helping prepare the ground for building a barn, carting, and making a bean rick.

His wife, Mary, was one of the two Rectory washerwomen, but she also turned her hand to winnowing, field work, helping the thatcher on a rick and dealing with smutty wheat. She served the Rectory on some 68 days in the year for a total of £1 4*s*. 6*d*., the basis of which being 3*d*. a day for most jobs. Thus this particular family in the year 1718 earned altogether £14 18*s*. 1*d*. – not very different from Gregory's figure – to which one should add a little for Richard's meals at harvest time. Nephew Jack was the Rector's ploughman on a wage of 3*d*. a day, and young Tom herded the Rector's pigs at pasture for several weeks, earning the considerable sum of 12*s*. 8*d*.

John Edmunds was Day's usual partner but, as we know, he stopped working for the Rector after the harvest, reappearing only once, in January, to sweep the Rectory chimneys. His place was taken by Charles Cannon, now on a man's wages, aged sixteen. As well as threshing and winnowing from October to the end of December, he did other outside jobs including digging a saw-pit needed for the timbers of the new barn. For his total of fifty days' work, he was paid £2 5*s*. 2*d*. – no doubt contributing to his widowed father at home and possibly saving a little with an eye to Ann White, the Rector's maid, whom he married five years later. John Edmunds's wife continued to work in the Rectory and in the fields, like Goody Day. In the year she earned 12*s*. 11*d*. and her husband only £6 6*s*. 0*d*., but one supposes that he also worked elsewhere. They were not a young couple, their two unmarried sons then being aged twenty and seventeen. Taking a full year's work by both Edmunds and his wife in 1717, they earned a total of £14 7*s*. 9*d*. I should make it absolutely clear that these taskers were paid weekly and the sums concerned so recorded; only at haymaking and harvest were wages paid to them in arrears.

From the concrete examples of Richard Day (1718) and John Edmunds (1717), it seems that Gregory King's estimated £15 a year for a labourer's family was normal for Lockinge. In effect, John Aldworth had, for his farm work – the source of his income – the services of two salaried men-servants, two nearly-full-time workers, a third throughout harvest, and a few other men and

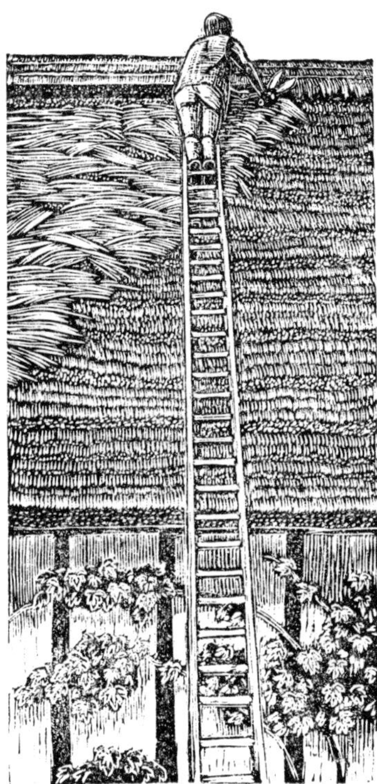

women occasionally. His total wage bill in 1718, covering all these categories, farm work and housework, was £42 10*s.* 4*d.* I have excluded specific work on building a barn and charges for a farrier's work. A man earned in one year roughly the cost of the Rector's annual hogshead of red wine – though, whether from abstinence or simple omission from the Accounts, 1718 is one of the few years in which wine purchases are not mentioned.

Having earlier stated the standard daily wage in Lockinge, which corresponds with that given for the south of England in *The Agrarian History of England*, one or two exceptions to this are worth mentioning. Some craftsmen – the thatcher, carpenter and builder – earned a regular 1*s.* 4*d.* a day; others, such as John Hitchcock who made and mended farm tools, James Tyler the collar-maker, and the local 'vet' John Ballard, were paid by the job – and well paid at that. Hitchcock charged a shilling for mending a sieve,

Ballard five shillings for drenching the Rector's horses; these specialists served the whole village or area. Certain field jobs done by women were rewarded on a piece-work basis. Setting beans and hoeing were both paid for at two shillings a land or acre, whereas weeding earned the standard woman's wage of 6*d.* a day. Old Elizabeth Cullam, a grandmother, earned quite large sums in most years, setting, hoeing or weeding crops for the Rector; in 1721, for example, she was paid £2 for hoeing ten acres twice – an enormous task. Perhaps the most pathetic payment (unless there was some covert explanation) was made each year to Goodman Bosely, parish clerk to the neighbouring 'Little' Hendred. He got threepence for 'wanting' Ardington Mead – in other words, setting traps for moles.

I have omitted two Account headings. 'Tithes', which were considered as part of Aldworth's farm income, and 'Taxes' which he treated not as farm expenses but as 'Other Expenses' to be deducted from the clear profit. Both will be discussed later.

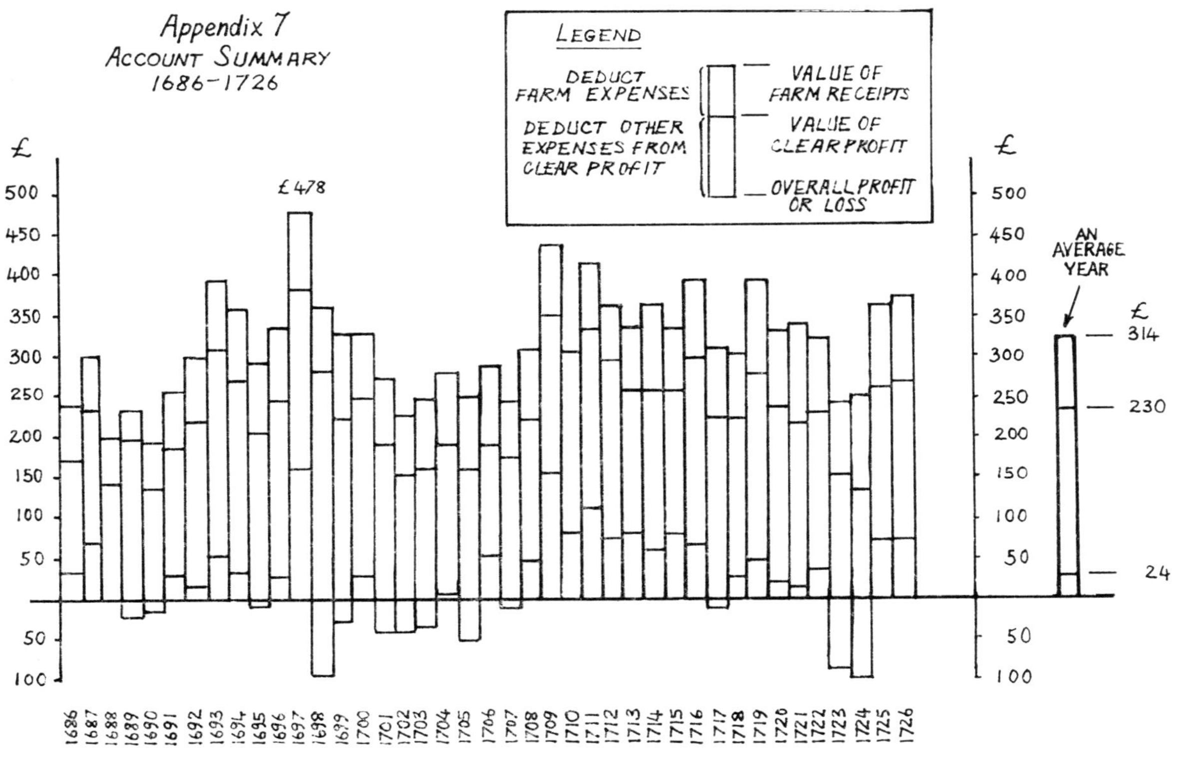
Appendix 7
ACCOUNT SUMMARY
1686–1726
LEGEND
DEDUCT FARM EXPENSES
DEDUCT OTHER EXPENSES FROM CLEAR PROFIT
VALUE OF FARM RECEIPTS
VALUE OF CLEAR PROFIT
OVERALL PROFIT OR LOSS
£
500
450
400
350
300
250
200
150
100
50
50
100
£478
1686
1687
1688
1689
1690
1691
1692
1693
1694
1695
1696
1697
1698
1699
1700
1701
1702
1703
1704
1705
1706
1707
1708
1709
1710
1711
1712
1713
1714
1715
1716
1717
1718
1719
1720
1721
1722
1723
1724
1725
1726
AN AVERAGE YEAR
£
314
230
24

CHAPTER SEVEN

The farming Rector: stable & backsides

JOHN ALDWORTH'S arable land was certainly his main source of income. His livestock were just as important; his horses provided his farm transport, bedded and fed from his own resources, and his pigs, cattle and poultry were the main items of Rectory diet. 'Backsides' was a separate heading in both Recepta and Expenses in the Accounts: the latter accounted for wages paid in pasturing the pigs and cows, the cost of buying and fattening stock, and the value of the Rector's own grain in this last action. Recepta only records what may be called by-products – the sale of stock, hides, skins and fat – and the occasional sale of eggs and milk. The result of accounting on these terms is that the backsides were certainly not an area of profit, but the Rector puts no value on the meat provided for his household from the slaughter of cattle, pigs and poultry. As shown in an earlier chapter, these amounts were considerable, feeding, as they did, a large household of Aldworth, his sister, two men-servants, two maids and, periodically, several extra taskers.

There was no Recepta heading for the stables; the Rector kept a separate record of the buying and selling of horses. Stable expenses are of course high, including as they do, the large amount of fodder and straw used. But horses were an absolute necessity to farming on any sort of a scale; it must have taken judgement to decide between keeping horses with all their expense and care, and hiring them. But then I do not suppose that they were always available for hire.

To return to the backsides. Perhaps the most important animal kept by the Rector, and by almost all smallholders, was the pig. It really did ensure the survival of mankind, for these reasons: a sow yielded a large farrow fairly quickly and the flesh of hogs could be salted and then hung up for future consumption; the Rector kept his for up to six months. Thus the necessary number of pigs could be slaughtered singly at fortnightly intervals, then hung up for about a month afterwards in January and February as flitches and finally taken down to eat, flitch by flitch, between April and October, the last one having been hung for about seven months. The Rectory needs for this period were five hogs and a sow and these were regularly slaughtered each December, the sow always being the last. Bacon was not the only meat to be eaten between April and October, but I think some readers will be as surprised as I was that salted and dried meat was not the winter diet, but was eaten right through the season of maximum work in the fields. Preserving meat of course saved the fodder needed otherwise to keep these animals alive.

A Rectory sow was usually put to boar, at a neighbouring farm, in November to provide a farrow of perhaps twelve piglets in spring. By May, a Mr Wilder (who is not met elsewhere in the Accounts) came to 'cut' some of the Rectory herd of pigs; though 'cutting' is a word used by Aldworth to mean 'killing and butchering', Mr Wilder's charges rather suggest neutering the animals. He dealt with seven or eight of them, always including a sow and he charged 4*d.* a sow, 3*d.* a sow pig and 1*d.* a boar pig. After this, in August or September, the pigs, now numbering about thirteen, 'went afield' under the supervision of a boy such as Tom Day who did this work every year from the age of nine to sixteen when he no doubt sought more permanent work elsewhere. The wage for this was 2*s.* a week and no nonsense: young Joseph Winterborne, taking Tom Day's place for some reason in 1719 at the age of ten, kept four hogs and eight pigs afield for six weeks and two days but 'I pd nothing for the 2 days Because one Hog was lame & kept at Home for above 2 weeks.' Those animals chosen for slaughter in December were then fattened on barley.

The Rector, perhaps because his infirmities kept him more indoors, began to make detailed notes of the dates on which his pigs were killed, hung up and finally taken down, and he used a simple code to identify each flitch. The two flitches of the first hog carried no mark; the second pair had a nail mark on the foreleg: the third a nail mark on the hind leg: the fourth two nail marks on the foreleg and so on.

There remained the necessity to provide meat for the rest of the year and to offer a change from a diet of dried meat. To deal with this, two or three calves were slaughtered in April and May and the veal supplied would supplement the bacon during the busy months of farming. In winter, perhaps two pigs and another calf would be killed to cover the months in which no bacon was available. Exactly what was eaten fresh and what was salted is not known, but there were purchases of salt by the sack and mention of brine tubs. Each year, with rare exception, the Rector has a bull slaughtered in November after some ten weeks' fattening with a neighbouring farmer, but the evidence in the Accounts suggests that this meat, or part of it, was given to poor parishioners; commonsense as well as charity would prompt this action to dispose of such a large quantity of beef. In 1719, shortly after his bull was killed, John Aldworth records:

'5 Dec. To 6 families in Ginge; they had no part in my bull – 6*s*'

And in the following year there is a similar entry. Both suggest that the Rector, faced with the enormous quantity of meat yielded by a bull's carcass, made a gift of much of it to the local poor; in these two cases he must have run out of beef before satisfying the last 'customer'. One may assume that in other years, in which no such entries occurred, the gifts continued but the rationing was more accurate. A shilling's-worth of beef would have been a sizeable amount.

His small herd of cattle went to pasture twice in the year from the confines of the backside, in spring and again in the autumn, on common pasture either on the Downs or at Laines – a name still in use north of Lockinge. Richard Tame looked after them (four or five cows) and was paid 4*d.* a cow when at Laines and 13*d.* a cow on the Downs where straying was a good deal more likely. Finally, at various times in the year to meet demand, a heifer or a cow was slaughtered; this was counterbalanced by the occasional purchase of stock and a bull was bought each May at a local market. The Rector used the sort of names for his cows that one might expect: 'Old Black', 'Cherry' and 'Broadhorns'. The shilling paid to Rob Absolom for each slaughter obviously included butchery into joints – yet another skill of this man of all trades. The killing of pigs and poultry carried no such reward.

Though meat was the first purpose of raising cattle, the Rectory was supplied with milk – though not with cream, which was usually bought – milking being the duty of the Rector's maid. Goody Hobbs sold butter to the Rectory (readers may remember that it cost 6*d*. a lb) and there is a rare mention of buying cheese which rather suggests that this was normally made at the Rectory. Another product of slaughter was the leather provided by the hides of bulls and cows and the skins of calves; these were sold and it is not known where the tanning was done. Calf skin was, of course, very often used for making gloves. Lastly, huge quantities of fat resulted from killing up to fifteen animals a year and this was also sold, some of it being used as tallow for the Rectory candles.

Being largely for home consumption, there are few entries in the Accounts about the poultry yard. Birds are regularly bought to keep up the numbers; the arrival of a family is once recorded when nineteen chicks and a hen were bought for 16*d*. There is no direct evidence of a Christmas turkey, but the Accounts would not include the killing of home-raised poultry; a Michaelmas goose does, however, appear at the appropriate time as the Rector does not raise his own geese. Eggs were of course available to the house and any surplus was sold.

Not so far mentioned is the very large amount of fodder required by stock in the backside. Aldworth's pigs had to be fed on home-grown beans and peas for much of the year; they ate perhaps a dozen quarters of these in a year, and those which were fattened consumed another five bushels of barley. Because I do not know exactly how many animals were kept by the Rector at any given time, it is not possible to say how many he allowed to be kept over the winter; but it must have been difficult to judge between the need for fresh meat and the drain on the crops used for fodder.

Escaping stock have always been a problem to farmers and their neighbours and John Aldworth noted one or two of these incidents in his *aide-mémoire*. His animals tended to escape from Barton Close and a heifer once reached Charlton on the outskirts of Wantage before recapture; another escaped twice in one year. Of the second of these the Rector notes:

'Red heifer broke out again & was bulld by Mr Plots' bull. Due to his maid – 1 shilling.'

Other parishioners also offended, such as Rob Mills, the Rector's neighbour, whose hogs did damage to the latter's property until 'his little maids' chased them into the village pound. Escaping again, they were once more impounded by Rob Absolom who then set off to obtain advice from the attorney, Mr Boot the elder. He was told 'that it being an open pound, we were neither obliged to drive them to the Hundred pound nor to feed them in the pound wherein they were. That if Rob Mills would not feed them nor pay the Damages nor replevy them, They must starve.' (To replevy was to restore distrained goods to their owner subject to the right to try the case at law.) Overcome by this learned counsel, Rob Mills paid half a guinea – ten shillings for the damage as assessed by two local farmers and sixpence for a peck of barley given to the hogs in the pound.

All in all, the backside, though ostensibly a loss in the Rector's Accounts, was actually the indispensable provider of his household's needs in meat. The wages bill is low because the servants did the work, but no credit is given for the value of the meat provided. Further detail of the values of stock, fodder and produce is given at the end of the chapter, in Appendix 8. Meanwhile one annual item in the backside expenses is given now for which I have no explanation in spite of seeking advice from experts.

Every year, except 1718 and 1720, there is an expense item for 'hurdles and combe bullocks'. Occasionally the two items are separated and detailed; thus: '12 hurdles at $3\frac{1}{2}$*d.* each and combe bullocks at one shilling a cow.' The 'rate per cow' varies each year, ranging from $10\frac{1}{4}$*d.* to 13*d.* and the number of cows from four to six. I can only suggest that the costs refer to pounding some of the Rector's cows so that they could be put to bull: in one year mention is made of carrying the hurdles off the Downs, which perhaps tells us where all this took place.

Another large claim on the Rector's crops came from the stable. As I said earlier, it is not possible to say exactly how many horses were kept by the Rector. Their purchase and sale are recorded under 'Ex Ex' and even these are irregular in time and number; one horse is kept for years, another for a few months. John Aldworth certainly had need of horses; a riding horse for himself and carthorses for his wagons, though the latter could be – and sometimes were – hired from other farmers for journeys to Streatley. There are, however, a few clues; the taxes paid by John Aldworth will be seen later, but one of them was a tax on horses 'for the King's carriages' levied on the number kept by an owner. In 1717 and 1718 this shows that the Rector paid for five and four horses respectively. Another clue is that in 1716 the Accounts show that, in fetching the coal from Streatley, he hired two horses and used four of his own. In my opinion it is likely that John Aldworth kept four working horses and a nag to ride himself, but nowhere in the Accounts is there mention of a special breed of horse to work the ploughs, carry heavy loads or bring in the harvests.

Every autumn, the Rector's grain was delivered by cart to corn-dealers, all within a day's journey of Lockinge, either with his own horses or by hiring or both. The Streatley journey for coal every year to collect over six tons of coal was usually done by hiring complete teams from his neighbours and this cost him no less than eight shillings per team of horse, wagon and carter; each team would carry a chaldron of coal – some 25½ hundredweight – and, when delivering corn, forty bushels thereof. The question every farmer faced was whether each and every working horse was worth the large quantities of feed consumed, the blacksmith's and the harness-makers' bills. The Rector's livestock – horses, cattle, pigs and poultry – were fed from his own crops; under half of his crops of beans and peas went to his stock and a little of his barley to fattening pigs. But all his oats – and he was sometimes forced to buy extra – were used at home in the stable. Similarly, a large amount of his own hay and of his tithe hay went to the backside too.

'Stabulum' was quite easily the largest item of farm expense and feed was the bulk of that item. Another very rough guide to the number of horses in the Rectory stable is to use Mavor's estimate (admittedly made over a century later) that a working horse will get through about fifty bushels of feed a year. Using this formula for a typical year such as 1725, the 250 bushels of oats, beans and peas laid up for the stable would suggest five horses.

As to other stable expenses, John Aldworth did not employ extra hands, so one may assume that his men-servants looked after the horses. He paid a quarterly account to Thomas Curtis, the village blacksmith, thus no details of this work or its costs are known. The trade of blacksmith certainly ran in the Curtis family; Thomas's father, who died in 1702, was himself a blacksmith and his uncle Robert was another, living at Ogbourne St. George in Wiltshire. Thomas was himself that rare Lockinge man, a bachelor householder; aged thirty-four in 1718, he lived with his widowed mother, Jane Curtis (she did not die until 1734), his brother John and his sister Mary. He often did a couple of days harvesting for the Rector. His cottage (these details come from the inventory to his father's will) contained, downstairs, the blacksmith's shop, a hall, buttery and brew-house: above these were four chambers. The lease of it was worth £10 and, like most villagers, he kept a few pigs in the backside. There were other visiting specialists, not all Lockinge parishioners, who probably served several villages. John Ballard occasionally dressed or drenched an injured or sick animal (using 'Marcom's balls' on one occasion as purveyed by Mr Lockton, the Wantage doctor); his brother James was the local wheelwright. The collarmaker did a great deal of repair work to harness, halters and leatherwork. These men were paid by the job, including materials, and repairs to large farming equipment were expensive: a new wagon bed cost £2 18*s.* 6*d.*: a set of wheels £4 19*s.* 0*d.*: a complete cart harness £4 10*s.* 0*d.* and Mr Bowles's second-hand wagon £4 6*s.* 0*d.* – but by far the most entries concerned minor repairs. No wonder that horses were the exclusive property of farmers rather than labourers.

As well as repairs to harness and wagons, other farm equipment needed frequent repair; in particular the wire and hair sieves often required 'bottoming' by John Hitchcock. A winnowing fan was an expensive item; the necessary wood to make it cost eleven shillings, and Thomas Robinson charged another nine shillings to complete the job. It is interesting that quite major parts of farming equipment were locally made; elm was cut for making a harrow; an ash tree was cut down and some of its timber used for a plough body. It seems from the Accounts that the timber for these two jobs was prepared locally and that they were finished by a skilled carpenter.

The expenses heading 'Reparations' not only reveals many of the

Rector's buildings but covers, like the backside expenses, many repairs to chicken troughs, cow and stable racks, ladders and gates. This is, perhaps, a good moment to emphasise two facts which emerge from studying John Aldworth's Accounts; the degree of self-sufficiency in repairing rather than replacing farm equipment and the many skills found among the village people of those days. These jobbing craftsmen were paid by the day, sometimes including diet, sometimes not, but usually at a higher rate than the labourer. William Winterborne, for example, was a carpenter, joiner and painter whom the Rector normally paid 1*s*. 4*d*. a day – 4*d*. more than the tasker. His sons followed him in his trade; Thomas, the elder, earned 8*d*. a day as a lad of sixteen while Will, his younger brother, got 6*d*. a day when he started helping his father at the age of fifteen. Thomas Robinson, who was not a Lockinge man, did similar work for the Rector. Both men could handle bricklaying jobs.

It is as well that they could because, in these last ten or so years of John Aldworth's life, most of the backside buildings were renewed or replaced. Understandably – but unfortunately for us – major work is recorded in the Accounts by the settling of a single bill, giving no detail covering wages. Luckily the materials were bought separately so that a great deal is known about the cost of them. In 1716, the Rector must have found serious rot in the footings of his barley barn in Barton Close. Robinson, with two mates, raised and propped its timber frame. Either this work was ineffective or a second barn was deemed necessary for work started on another, after some necessary preliminaries, about two years later. This work again shows how local men and local materials were so often used; firstly, a sawpit was dug and then, a month later, Thomas Smith provided the transport for five loads of the Rector's timber to Barton Close. In 1719, he again helped lift no less than seventeen loads to the same place at a cost of three shillings a load. One can therefore picture the necessary timber being shaped and prepared for erection on site by the carpenters. This new barn shows an interim phase between the old timber-framed structure with wattle and daub infilling and the future structure built of bricks. The Rector's barn was still timber-framed but it was infilled with brick and roofed in tiles. Although little can be deduced from a general bill of £33 4*s*. 8¼*d*., some idea of the barn's length comes from the use of thirty-six ridge tiles. Later, paving tiles were put down at its north and south ends, requiring no less than 1,100 of them.

There then followed a new cart-house (over £13) and wood-house (£14) and repairs to the milk-house, coach-house and bottle-house; few of us probably have any idea of how many bricks or tiles go to an average house, but it is worth recording that John Aldworth bought over 6,700 bricks and nearly 10,000 tiles between 1716 and 1728. The carrying of these heavy loads was extremely expensive; a purchase of 1,000 bricks from Mr Crips, for example, cost fifteen shillings which is exactly the price asked for their carriage from the Downs to Lockinge by Thomas Smith's horses.

As he was involved in all this rebuilding as well as being a frequent help with the Rector's ricks, it is time to introduce Richard Toms, the local thatcher. Like his fellow-craftsmen the carpenters, Toms commanded a higher rate of daily pay; he could not and did not work alone. His team consisted of himself (1*s*. 4*d*. a day), his server (1*s*. a day) and his two elmers, who were women, on 6*d*. a day. Though the thatcher was essential for roofing some buildings – tiles were beginning to replace thatch – he was usually a part-time worker and Richard was no exception; appropriately he was also a barber. As well as buildings to work on, there were also ricks to be thatched almost every year. The word 'elmer' perhaps needs some explanation: these assistants were necessary to prepare the long straw wheat thatch, firstly by wetting the straw to make it pliable and then by gathering the straw into bunches about eighteen inches wide and five inches deep. These are commonly called 'yealms' and are then put together in a Y-shaped yoke for the thatcher.

At the end of the chapter, in Appendix 8, is a list of the materials used for building in the Rectory backside, of farmyard items mentioned and of the local brick kilns. Costs are added whenever possible. Secondly, further details are given of livestock in the backside and the foodstuffs needed to keep them.

Appendix 8

BUILDING, BACK SIDE AND STABLE ITEMS MENTIONED

1. **Building materials**	*Cost*
Building bricks	100 for 1*s*. 6*d*.–2*s*.
Paving bricks	100 for 2*s*. 1*d*.–2*s*. 6*d*.
Hair	10*d*. a bushel
Laths	100 for 1*s*. 6*d*.–2*s*. 6*d*.
Lath nails	1,000 for 1*s*. 6*d*.–1*s*. 8*d*.
Ledgers	Not known
Lime	6*d*.–8*d*. a bushel
Nails	Not known
Dowel pins	Not known
Sprays	100 for 3½*d*.–4*d*.
Hip tiles	Not known
Roofing tiles	100 for 1*s*. 6*d*.–1*s*. 10*d*.
Ridge tiles	3½*d*. each
Red sand	Not known
Red pitching stones	Not known

2. **Timber**	
'Board'	200ft cost £1. 3*s*. 0*d*. (over 2½*d*. a ft)
Elm board	36ft cost 3*s*. (1*d*. per ft)
	31ft cost 3*s*. 6*d*. (under 1½*d*. per ft)
Oaken tops	23ft cost 15*s*. 4*d*. (8*d*. per ft) meaning unknown

4. **Paint**	
Linset oil	1*s*. 1*d*. a quart
Red oker	1*s*. 6*d*. a lb
Whiting	1*d*. a lb

4. **Farmyard items**			
Bridle	3*s*. 6*d*. each	Girth	1*s*. each
Lantern	3*s*. 4*d*.	Cartline	About 7*s*.
Stable brooms	1*s*. a dozen	Scythe	2*s*. 6*d*.
Sieve	About 3*s*.	Barn shovel	1*s*. 6*d*.

5. **Kilns mentioned**

Latin Downe Hatteridge Ore	The Rector called them 'kills'. As well as substantial purchases from them, he sold wheat straw to them in some years.

THE RECTORY BACKSIDE FURTHER DETAILS AND COSTS

1. **Livestock**

Bulls: It seems that the Rector kept a bull for about eighteen months, buying in April or May for between £2. 10*s*. 0*d*. and £3. 11*s*. 0*d*. and slaughtering it in November of the year following. No bull was sold.

Cows: Over the ten years only three cows, each with a calf, were bought (£3. 3*s*. 0*d*.–£3. 17*s*. 6*d*.); whereas a total of ten were sold over this period at slightly lesser prices (£2. 10*s*. 0*d*. –£3. 6*s*. 8*d*.).

Heifers: Over ten years eleven were bought (£1. 16*s*. 0*d*.–£3. 6*s*. 0*d*.) and only one was sold for £3. 0*s*. 0*d*.

Calves: The Rector raised his calves from his own cows so none was ever bought. Occasionally a calf was sold for about £1, including Black Tag's calf which, at the age of five weeks and one day, fetched nine shillings. Apart from slaughtering his calves for meat, the Rector sometimes bought a shoulder of veal.

Pigs: Only once did the Rector buy any pigs. Seven of them, cut and weaned, cost him £2. 13*s*. 0*d*.

Markets: Though John Aldworth does not always record where he bought or sold stock, local town markets such as Newbury, Abingdon and Faringdon are mentioned.

2. **Other produce**

Hides: A bull's hide fetched between six and fourteen shillings, a cow's eight to ten shillings, and a steer's nine to twelve shillings. A calf skin was worth 2½*d*. a pound weight and in one recording, two such skins weighed 47lbs. All were sold very soon after slaughter but to whom is not known.

Poultry: Typical buying prices for live birds were: goose 30*d.*; turkey 2*s.* 6*d.*–3*s.* 6*d.*; duck 9*d.* Eggs were sold when surplus to Rectory needs but only the value, not the quantity, is given.

3. **Foodstuffs for stock**

Quantities varied but the following, taken from one year, 1725, are typical. Their total value was £9. 12*s.* 0*d.*

Barley: 10 bushels at 25 shillings were laid up for hogs and poultry in April at the start of the year.

Beans: 36 bushels, worth £3. 12*s.* 0*d.*, were laid up for the hogs in late November and early December.

Peas: These were fed to the hogs after the beans were finished and were eaten until the end of January. 24½ bushels, worth £4. 15*s.* 0*d.*, were laid up.

General: The storage of grain was a problem and is studied in the next chapter. It is sufficient to say at this point that grain was often stored for one or even two years before being used as foodstuff for stock. Use was made of ricks, barns (where threshing and winnowing was carried out), granaries and finally garners, from which the animals' food was taken daily.

CHAPTER EIGHT

Tithes and taxes 1716-1729

NEITHER of these subjects is compellingly interesting to most people and learned books have been written about both. I shall confine myself largely to John Aldworth's tithes, which reveal a great deal about his parishioners, and leave a summary of both tithes and taxes to an appendix.

All of us know that a tithe is a tenth part and that some clergy were entitled to collect this fraction of a parishioner's income in cash or in kind; in fact, by John Aldworth's time they had become much more complex than that. Collection, even in a small parish, must have been a laborious affair and this may well explain why the Rector employed a 'tithing man' until 1702. Not only was the income from Lockinge tithes significant – if perhaps not great – but the Rector, no doubt, considered it his duty to collect them as a proper tribute to Holy Church. In 1718 the following tithes were collected:

		£	s	d
Petty tithes	Mainly covering livestock & fruit Cash taken with some kind.	4	4	4½
Easter Offerings	A small levy in cash on every parishioner of adult age.	0	18	1
Hay	Taken in cash and kind. Amounted to about	23	0	0
Sheep per moneth	Cash tithe on sheep pastured.	1	17	7
Wooll	A literal tithe of one fleece for every ten sheared in the parish.	12	0	0
	Total tithe value:	£42	0	0½

An approximate figure is given for Hay as Aldworth includes both tithe receipts and the value of his own hay under the heading. The figure for wooll (spelt thus it seems much warmer) represents the sale of 104 tithe fleeces received that year, weighing eleven tod – just over 300lb – and sold in Newbury for £11. 11*s* 0*d*.; the extra 9*s*. was for the remainder of the 1717 wooll. Noticeable is the complete absence of tithe on grain crops which were, of course, the farmers' chief source of wealth. On the other hand, John Aldworth's tithes rightly fell on the better-off, leaving the poorest to contribute an Easter Offering of perhaps 5*d*.; this is what John Pisie, a landless labourer paid in 1718 – and John Aldworth often forgave the poorest parishioners even that contribution – compared with Mr Charles Collins's total contribution of over £6 in tithes and Thomas Church's, then farming 22 acres, of under 12 shillings. Apart from the value to John Aldworth, tithe receipts, when related to all other evidence, offer a great deal of detail about Lockinge families. The Easter Offering – which was a due, not an offering – is recorded in the Accounts using a simple code of abbreviations. 'W', 'br', 'D' or 'dr' and 'son' are all easily decoded but only the very occasional full writing of 'Garden' reveals the meaning of 'G'. The following extract from the 1718 Easter Offering will explain the matter:

'William Munt	son, dr, G	7*d*
His servants	1 pd	2*d*
Thomas Curtis	Mo, Br, sis, G	9*d*
Jonathan Curtis	G	3*d*
Thomas Kimber	W [*deleted*] G	5*d*'

Using all the evidence available, the above can be expanded as follows: William Munt, widowed the previous year and farming over 400 acres, paid 2*d*. each for himself and his grown-up son and daughter, with a penny more for his garden. Like Charles Collins, he paid over £6 in total tithes that year. Thomas Curtis, aged thirty-four years, blacksmith, lived in his late father's house (his father died in 1702) with his old mother, a brother and a sister – who cannot be identified as he had two of each. He had a garden but no other land and paid no other tithe.

Jonathan Curtis, a young man married in 1713 but widowed in 1717 (hence John Aldworth's deletion of a *W* against his name) and left with a son, now aged four; having no land or garden, contributed a total of 3*d*. He was not directly related to Thomas Curtis.

The entry opposite Thomas Kimber – 'W G' – is far more typical in the Easter Offering. He was the village tailor who, with his wife Margaret, was unusual in having a family of girls only; two had been born by 1718 and another two were to follow in 1719 and 1721. One should perhaps add that 'Garden' probably meant a piece of ground in which vegetables grew or a few stock and poultry were raised.

A few other interesting facts come from the Easter Offering. In 1718, it includes thirty-one couples, the remaining ten persons being nine widowers or bachelors and one widow – Tomasina or Tomsie Yates.

The basis of the hay tithe is too difficult for me. I suspect that there were complicated agreements, altered and modified over the years, between the Rector and each owner. The following extract will make my point. In 1719, Thomas Smith paid these hay tithes:

5 acres & 1 yard Ditchmead at 2*s*. an acre	10*s*. 6*d*.
1 acre & 3 yards Middlemead at 2*s*. 6*d*. an acre	4*s*. 4½*d*.
1 acre & 1 yard Long Dole at 5*s*. an acre	6*s*. 3*d*.

All that can be deduced from this is that four yards equalled one acre.

Details of the two sheep tithes tell us who locally owned the sheep, the size of their flocks, and current wool prices in Newbury. All told there must have been about 1,000 Lockinge sheep on the Downs, though this figure drops towards 1729; a flock of 200–300 was usual. Berkshire was then well known for its short wool of high quality suitable for cloth, as opposed to the long wool for worsted. Its price in 1716–29 varied from over £1 a tod in 1718 down to 12*s*. 6*d*. or 13*s*. later. An enjoyable extract from John Aldworth's 1719 Account entry for Wooll, showing a keen eye for business is:

'11 July. Sold Mr Fourd 10 Tod½ of wooll for £9.17.0. I was to have had 30*d* more, But this was remitted upon His carrying away the wooll on his owne Horse.

After I had received money for wooll, Goody Hobbs told me Her husband had 20*s* a Tod & a Guinea over.'

Tax, very much a going concern in John Aldworth's day, was basically levied by the Government on land holding, not on income. The main one was Land Tax, first applied in 1692, which levied a quota from each county; thereafter, Commissioners – and John Aldworth was one for many years – broke down the county quota to parish and finally individual levies at so much in the pound value of land. This tax formed about three quarters of the Rector's annual tax bill: paid quarterly, the amount varied though seeming to stay steady for five-year periods. Further details of this and of other taxes paid between 1716 and 1729 are given at Appendix 9. These, as may be seen, included ecclesiastical taxation, though of a fairly minor nature.

One might expect that tax collection would be in the hands of the more important parishioners, but this was not so. The Land Tax and Window Tax were collected by one person, a smallholder such as Thomas Cullam of Ginge, or later, by his son John whom we have met as the Rector's servant for a short period and who also witnessed his will. The Poor Tax was handled by an overseer or his deputy and these posts changed hands more often. The extraordinary tax levied for the king's horses or carriages was collected in 1718 by 'the constable' – the only mention of this village dignitary in the Accounts. Highway Tax, understandably, was dealt with by one of the tenant farmers, as the owner of transport and a major road-user. Whether he actually saw to the repairs to roads, having delivered the load of flints, is not known.

If one relates John Aldworth's annual tax payments of all sorts to his annual farm income – which was not of course the basis of taxation – it may be said that about a tenth of his income went in both civil and ecclesiastical taxation.

Appendix 9

Some Details of the Rector's Tithes and Taxes

TITHES

Petty Tithes

Cows & calves: The tithe appears to be based on a variable rate per beast that is killed or sold. A tithe of 2*d.* is levied on each cow, regardless of its value. In the case of calves and weaners, a tithe of roughly one tenth of its selling price was raised (e.g. a 10*d.* tithe raised on two calves sold for 9*s.*). Sometimes the tithe is paid in kind – such as a shoulder of veal. It also seems that a halfpenny tithe was paid for each calf weaned. As will be seen, this was a complicated matter with a low yield; in 1718, twenty-six shillings and elevenpence was collected from twenty-eight owners, of whom eight had no cause for payment and one paid in kind.

Pigs: Curiously few tithes were collected – only four people paid in 1718, all in cash, as the Rector owned his own pigs – and the basis seems again to have been one tenth of selling price.

Lambs: Again, the tithe seems to be one tenth of the value of each lamb born. For example, a 15*s.* tithe was paid on 90 lambs sold for 20*d.* each.

Fruit & orchards: Five persons paid a tithe on fruit in 1718. It was in this case based on one twentieth of the selling price or paid in kind. The sale of an orchard invoked the same penalty – one sold for £10 being tithed at 10*s.*

Hops: One or two farmers grew hops, including Mr Charles Collins, and the tithe was one twelfth of the sale price. Thus Mr Collins once delivered 3lb of hops to the Rector (which the latter needed for brewing) on 36lb of hops sold. Hops also carried a Government tax.

Pigeons: The bigger farmers kept pigeon houses, that most ancient of devices for ensuring continuous fresh meat, and though the basis of the tithe is not known to me, payments show that a pigeon was then valued at a penny. Mrs Mary Smith of Alleblasters, in 1718, paid 3*s.* for 'spring pigeons' in June and another 2*s.* 6*d.* for 'Autumne pigeons'.

Egs (as then spelt): These incurred a tithe but, again, a surprisingly small number of people paid it – five in 1718. Such sums as two shillings were paid; Mrs Ansty preferring to mix cash with kind when she gave the Rector one shilling and seventeen eggs. Many others probably kept poultry but did not sell the eggs.

Easter Offering: Paid by the head of every family at a rate of twopence per adult, including servants and adult relations in the house; and of one penny for a garden.

Great Tithes

Hay: I am quite unable to work out a basis for the various assessments. A given close would yield a certain tithe each year – many were 1*s*. 6*d*. – in terms of its size, not yield. Every hayfield seemed to have a different tithe, sometimes a good deal more than 1*s*. 6*d*. Thomas Cullam, for example, paid £1. 5*s*. 0*d*. annually on the Laines.

Sheep per moneth: This heading included the small payments for the number of sheep pastured in the parish. It normally worked out at twopence per ten sheep per month; a useful added piece of information is a list of such farmers who employed shepherds. John Aldworth paid each according to flock size – Mr Collins's shepherd was paid 2*s*. 6*d*., presumably for his information.

Wooll: A straightforward tithe of one fleece for every ten wintered in the parish. The fleeces were collected after the shearing in June and sold, often at Newbury. In 1718, for example, the Rector received 104 fleeces in tithe which were sold at Newbury in July to Mr Ford for £11. 11*s*. 0*d*., the wool amounting to eleven tod in weight (1 tod weighed 28lb or 2 stone).

TAXES

Land Tax: This was based on land value and the actual rate during the period in question is not known. The tax was paid quarterly and varied between 1716 and 1729. In the first of these years it stood at £7. 11*s*. 2¾*d*. a quarter, but then dropped to £6. 4*s*. 8*d*. from 1717–21; there was then a further fall to £4. 3*s*. 1*d*. from 1722–7, followed – though these last Accounts are confused – by about £6 or £7 a quarter.

Poor Tax: Judging from one entry (1728) the rate was also based on land value. In that year the Rector paid 8*s*. 6*d*. at 6*d*. in the £ but from the figures for other years this may only have been a quarter's contribution.

Highways: An annual payment of 8*s*. 6*d*. (perhaps another 6*d*. in the £) with an occasional contribution of flints for which cartage was payable. The Laines is mentioned as the destination for stones in 1726, probably for the road going eastward from Wantage.

The King's Carriages: Levied in only three years of the thirteen concerned. In 1717 at 6*d*. a horse owned; in 1718 at 3*d*. and in 1728, at 9*d*. Possibly a special levy to improve the roads locally for the King's passage. Useful for research as it reveals the number in the Rectory stable.

Windows: Two half-yearly payments of 15*s*. This should disclose the number of windows in the Rectory but the rate varied periodically after its introduction in 1696, and is not known for the years discussed.

Candles: A straight tax of one penny per pound weight of candles. The Rector paid an average of six shillings a year; whether it was levied on the poorest villager is not known.

Haywards: This curious-sounding tax was in fact a levy towards the upkeep of parish hedges. John Aldworth paid it only twice – 6*s*. in 1727 and 5*s*. 7½*d*. in 1728.

Gaol money: Whether there was a village lock-up is not known and the Rector paid 3½*d*. 'jaole money' in two years: 1727 and 1728.

ECCLESIASTICAL LEVIES

Tenths: Since 1704 this levy had been paid into Queen Anne's Bounty, a fund to increase the poorer stipends of clergy; Bishop Burnet of Salisbury had been one of its proposers. John Aldworth contributed three guineas a year, due at Christmas but often paid later.

Archdiaconal Levy: Sometimes referred to by Aldworth as 'synodals and procurations' and which amounted to 11*s*. 2*d*.

annually for Lockinge. Mr Price sometimes represented John Aldworth in presenting the levy in which case his expenses were paid: 'Allowed him for his dinner etc – 5*s* 4*d*'.

Bishop's Visitations: These took place about every two years, though the Accounts do not usually tell us where. In 1723 a visitation took place at Wallingford. The normal levy was 6*s*. 10½*d*.

Easter Offrings (33)

Harmer Reading, G — X 05

His servts — 2 P — X 04

Jos Cutler, W, S, G — X 07

Jos Cropp, W, G forgiven X — X 05

Jos Kew, W, G — X 05

John Yalie, W, A — X 04

Jos Adams, W, G — — 05

Wm Mackal, W, G — — 05

Harmer Mant, Son, D, G — X 07

His servts 1 P — X 02

Mr Collins, W, G — X 05

His servts — 4 P — X 08

Hr Yales, Ha, W, G — X 07

Tho Church, W, G — X 05

Tho Cutler, W, Si, D, G — X 07

Wm Smith, W, G — X 05

Ed Andy, W, G — — 05

His servts — —

Th Cutler, Mo, Br, Si, G — X 09

Wm Winterborne, W, G — X 05

Wm Snorsel, Son, Dr X

Jos Pipe, W, G — — 05

Tho Kimber, W, G — X 05

Jonathan Cutler, W, G — X 3 0[illegible]

Jos Pane, W, G — X 05

Wm Tubb, W, G — X 05

Henry Yaly, W, G — X 05

Tho Waker, W, G — X 05

Wm Hine, W, G — X 05

Wm Moulden, W — — 04

Jos Nokes, W, G — X 05

Jos Blackwell, W, G — X 05

Wm Oaly, W, G — X 00

Jos Blagram, G — — 05

Wil Yales, G — X 03

Hr Faine, W, G — X 05

Rich Cutler, W, G — X 05

Wm Smith, W, — 2 P — X 05

His servts — X 04

Tho Smith, W, G — — X 05

His servants 2 P — X 04

John Symmonds, W, D, G X 07

Wm Cannon, G — X 03

Tho Hobbs, W, G — X 07

His servants 1 P — X 02

Mr Rich Collins, W, maid — X 06

Mrs Anne, G — X 03

03 — 01

15 00

04. 04. 04 od

5 02 05 od

CHAPTER NINE

The Rector leaves his parish

1729 seems another normal year of John Aldworth's accounting – his forty-fourth year in Lockinge – but the handwriting has begun to straggle a bit and there are a few incorrect entries. The crops are sown, hoed and weeded while the grain of 1728 was still being threshed and winnowed in the Rectory barn by the faithful Richard Day and Jonathan Atkins. On the 7th of June, the Rector duly attended a meeting in Wantage on Land Tax business and on the 23rd of June, Day and Atkins 'came into the house' ready for haymaking. Sixty-four tithe fleeces had been collected after the shearing and the usual deliveries of five chaldrons of coal and a hogshead and a half of wine had taken place at the end of June. None of these entries suggest a dying man, but there are fewer in July. On the 17th of July Mr Towsy, the physician, was paid for 'ingredients' – obviously medicine of sorts – while Jonathan brewed the next barrel of Rectory beer. On the 20th of July comes John Aldworth's last entry: a sixpenny gift to a traveller with a pass. Aldworth had made a will in 1724 and it read as follows:

IN DEI NOMINE, AMEN.

I, John Aldworth Rector of the parish of East Lockinge in the County of Berks do make this my last Will in Manner and form following. First in all the humility of a contrite Heart I beg of God the pardon of all my sins through the Merritts and Mediation of Jesus Christ my only Saviour and though I have been a most prodigal son yet my Hope is in Christ that for his sake God my most merciful Creator will not cast off the Bowells of a most compassionate father to me. As to my faith I have lived and by God's grace intend to dye in the profession of the Catholick faith of Christ a true Member of his catholick Church in the Communion of a living part thereof the Church of England as it now stands by law established. I leave my Body to the Earth whence it was taken in full Assurance of the Resurrection to eternal life. I will have none invited to my funeral but such of my parish who are of age to communicate nor any provision made for them but Gloves only. I will have no velvet paul nor Escutcheons. I will be buried in the Church Yard at the Chancell end in a plain Coffin neither lined or faced. I desire the Solemnity may be finished by Noon. As to my worldly Estate, I give to my dear kinsman Gilbert Jackson Esq late of the county and City of Oxford the full sum of three hundred pounds of good and lawful Money of Great Brittaine to be paid to him or to his Heirs and Assigns by my Executrix hereinafter mentioned within twelve Months next after my decease. Item I give to six poor Men of my parish Twenty shillings each for carrying me themselves or by their substitutes to my Grave. Item I give Twenty pounds of lawful money of England to be divided between mine and my Sister's servants at the discretion of my Executrix. All the rest of my worldly Estate (my debts and funerall Expenses first payd) I do give to my dear sister Susanna Hester whom I do hereby appoint sole Executrix of this my last Will and Testament. In Witness whereof I have hereunto set my Hand and Seal 14 March 1724. Seald signed and declared in the presence of

Walter Hart John Cullam

John Aldworth died on the 24th of July 1729, just a month after his seventy-seventh birthday. Two days later he was buried – no doubt in the manner he had wished – and an entry made in the parish 'Burials in Woollen' book:

'Mr John Aldworth Rector of this Parish was buried and a certificate was brought within 8 days that he was buried in woollen only.

Seen and allowed by Charles Collins & Tho Garrard.'

The will reveals much of the man. It is forthright both in proclaiming religious belief and in rejecting funereal pomp; it makes provision for those for whom he cared most: Gilbert (Gillie) Jackson – whose name occurs in the Accounts from time to time – his sister Susanna, their servants and six poor parishioners. It would not be difficult to guess that John Noke was among the coffin-bearers.

During his lifetime, John Aldworth had acquired several small pieces of land in Lockinge and transferred them to All Soul's College for the benefit of future Rectors. His tomb is said (I quote the *History of East Lockinge*) to have had an inscription detailing a charity that he left to the village. The same book refers also to his leaving £6 to the deserving poor and £2 towards the parish clerk's small stipend. There is no record of these bequests, as can be seen, in his will. As to the inscription, this may well have been removed when his tomb was restored in 1853 by the then Rector, The Revd. Lewis Sneyd. It still lies under the east wall of the old chancel at Lockinge church and the inscription reads as follows:

In memory
of the Rev
John Aldworth
Rector of this
Parish in which he
resided 44 years
He died
July 24, 1729
This tomb was repaired
and renewed by the
Rector of Lockinge 1853

John Aldworth was replaced by Dr. Stephen Niblett who was inducted to the living on the 5th of September 1729. It was the latter who bore the brunt of Matthew Wymondsold's impact on the village. There is evidence that Dr. Niblett was severely harassed by the new lord of the manor who used a number of aggressive devices to get the Rectory moved elsewhere to make room for a new manor house. Niblett outlived his persecutor by some nine years, dying in 1766. Two years earlier he had given £500 towards the expenses of an Act of Parliament annexing the living of East Lockinge to the Wardenship of All Souls and this continued until 1873 when the Loyd family bought the advowson.

Susanna Hester did not long survive her brother, being buried in Lockinge in 1731. Two years later she was followed by Charles Collins, for so long a friend of his Rector.

INDEX